Tove Fevang

Totally Simple
Crochet

Over 30 Easy Projects for the Home and to Wear

T

TRAFALGAR SQUARE
North Pomfret, Vermont

First published in the United States of America
in 2011 by
Trafalgar Square Books
North Pomfret, Vermont 05053

Originally published in Norway in 2010
by Cappelen Damm AS

ISBN: 978-1-57076-474-5

Library of Congress Control Number: 2010943263

Photography (layout): Ragnar Hartvig
Detail Photos: Geir Arnesen
Styling: Ingrid Skaansar
Design: Lise Mosveen
Cover design: RM Didier

Printed in China

10 9 8 7 6 5 4 3 2 1

Table of Contents

Preface

Crochet is one of the easiest handcraft techniques I know of. All you need to get going is a crochet hook and a ball of yarn.

Some people regard crochet as just an old-fashioned craft. I certainly don't believe that, even though I learned to crochet from my grandmother when I was 5 or 6 years old. She always had a crochet project at hand. Since I was curious about anything handmade, all I had to do was to ask her in order to learn. It was a challenge for her to teach me because I was left-handed but she had a solution—I could learn how to hold the hook in my right hand. It wasn't easy at first but she had a couple of good reasons for teaching me that way.
I immediately understood the first reason. It was simply more comfortable to sit close to her on the sofa and crochet than to sit on the other side of the table in order to see what she did in reverse. In that case, I could have crocheted as she did but with the left hand. That was how my grandfather taught me to embroider. The other reason was that, if I crocheted from left to right and wanted to crochet following a pattern, I might have to read it mirror-image. Little by little, I learned how to crochet with my right hand.

With my interest in handcraft I realized early on that I wanted a textile and design education. Handwork is both my profession and one of my leisure interests. When evening comes and I am rather tired after a long workday, getting out the crochet hook and some yarn re-energizes me. Everything else melts away as I relax with my crocheting.

The purpose of this book is to inspire your creativity. If you haven't crocheted before, begin with the general information section of the book. It shows how the crochet stitches are formed and the structures they make. One of the most exciting aspects of crochet is the simplicity of combining stitch patterns. Feel free to change the colors or the yarn, combine techniques and make the piece your own. Today's market offers any yarn you could desire. You'll find many wonderful wool, alpaca, cotton, linen, and silk yarns in every weight and color. I often find the process of the project is more important than having the piece finished. It is certainly why I like always having something in my hands and it makes me happy when the result is just what I envisioned.

I have had a lot of excellent help with the projects in this book. My husband, Geir Arnesen, took all the step-by-step photos, working at all hours whenever the pieces were ready to be photographed. Berit Østlie helped me crochet some of the projects when I didn't have enough time. Ingrid Skaansar and Ragnar Hartvig styled and photographed, producing all of the lovely and inspirational pictures of the designs. Last, but not least, thanks to my publisher's editor, Inger Margrethe Karlsen, who believed in the project and made it possible to complete. Many thanks to everyone, without each and every one of you, it would not have been possible to make this book.

Best wishes, Tove
www.tovefevang.no

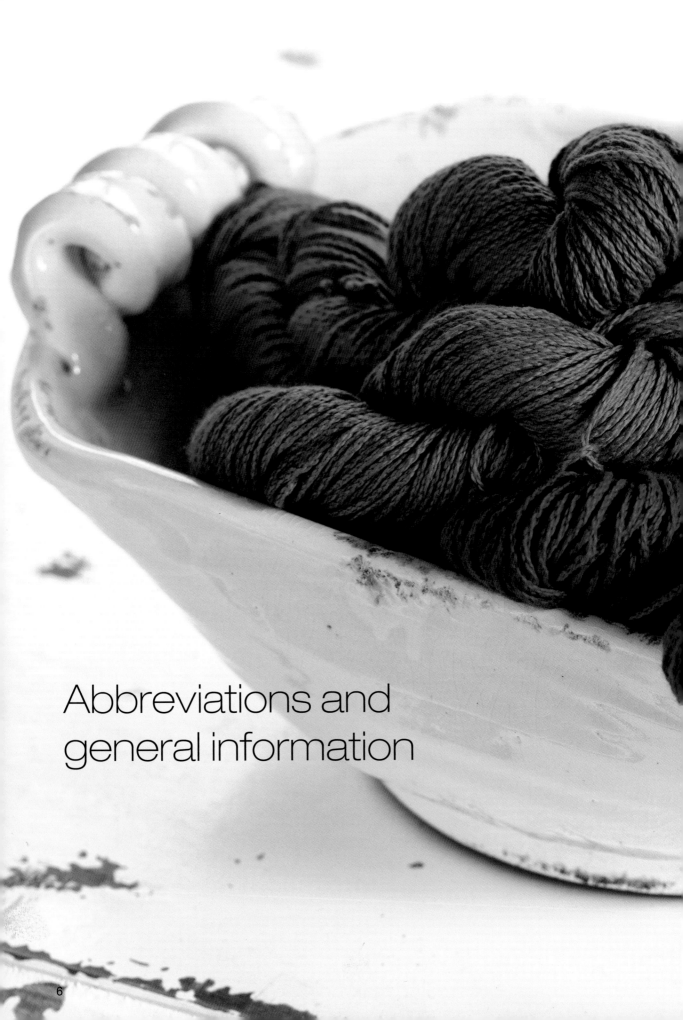

Abbreviations and
general information

Abbreviations:

beg = begin, beginning	**RS** = right side
ch = chain stitch	**sc** = single crochet
dc = double crochet	**sl st** = slip stitch
dbl tr = double treble	**st(s)** = stitch(es)
hdc = half double crochet	**tr** = treble
rep = repeat	**tog** = together
rnd = round	**WS** = wrong side

dc gr = double crochet group. Work the same number of double crochet stitches in the same stitch or over a chain loop as indicated by the number before "dc gr." For example 3-dc gr = 3 dc into the same stitch.

Clusters: Leave a loop on the hook from each of the stitches that will be joined into a cluster, plus a loop from the first stitch. Yarn around hook again and pull through all the stitches. A cluster can be crocheted with all types of double or treble crochet stitches that are worked as a group into the same stitch.

hdc cluster = half double crochet cluster. Work as many hdc into the same stitch as indicated by the number before the abbreviation, for example, 4-hdc cluster.

dc cluster = double crochet cluster. Work as many dc into the same stitch as indicated by the number before the abbreviation, for example, 4-dc cluster.

tr cluster = treble cluster. Work as many tr into the same stitch as indicated by the number before the abbreviation, for example, 4-tr cluster.

dbl tr cluster = Work as many dbl tr into the same stitch as indicated by the number before the abbreviation, for example, 3-dbl tr cluster.

Paired dbl tr cluster = paired double treble cluster. Work as many dbl tr into the same stitch as indicated by the number before the abbreviation, for example, paired 3-dbl tr cluster. Work as for a dbl tr cluster until the last step and leave all 3 dbl tr loops on the hook, skip 5 sc and then make another 3-dbl tr cluster, and end with yarn over hook and through all 6 loops on the hook so that 1 loop remains.

Crab stitch = single crochet worked from left to right.

Decrease 1 dc = Make 1 dc but stop when 2 loops remain on the hook. Make a stitch into the next st but stop when there are a total of 3 loops on the hook, yarn over hook and bring through all 3 loops. Decrease single and half double crochet sts the same way.

Increase 1 dc = Make 2 dc in the same stitch. Increase single or half double crochet sts the same way.

Check your gauge! If your stitch and row gauge doesn't match that in the pattern, try another size crochet hook. If your gauge is too tight, use a bigger hook; if it is too loose, use a smaller hook.

Chain stitch (ch):

Step 1: *Make a slip knot, insert hook into loop and bring yarn from the ball through the loop on the hook, tighten yarn to firm up the loop around the hook.*

Step 2: *Hold the hook in your right hand and the yarn over your left index finger. With yarn over the hook, bring hook through the loop already on hook and then you have a chain st (ch). Continue the same way until you have the desired number of stitches in the chain. Most crochet pieces begin with either a crochet chain or ring.*

Step 3: *If you are going to work with single crochet (sc), half double crochet (hdc), double crochet (dc), or treble crochet (tr), begin by inserting the hook into the chain st indicated in the pattern. First wrap the yarn the correct number of times around the hook for the stitch (the example here is once over the hook for a double crochet) and then insert the hook into the 4th chain from the hook and complete the stitch. The first 3 chain sts are counted as one dc.*

Step 4: *With yarn around hook, pull through loops until the stitch is completed and then work across the chain in pattern.*

Step 5: *Making a ring: Insert hook into the 1st chain (beg st) and pull yarn through both loops at the same time.*

Step 6: *Completed chain ring.*

Materials

In order to crochet you'll need a crochet hook sized appropriately for the yarn. You'll also need scissors and a blunt tapestry needle for sewing up. Crochet hooks are made from a variety of materials, including metal, plastic, bamboo, and wood. My favorite hooks are wood because they are easy to hold and very comfortable to work with. If you buy a set of hooks in sizes E-4 – N/P 15 / 3.5-10 mm, you'll always have a hook that suits your hand and it will be easy to find the right size for the desired yarn and gauge.

Beginning or Ending a Piece
Many patterns tell you to chain loosely. It's not always easy to do that and it's a good rule of thumb to use a larger size hook than that specified for the piece. For example, if the instructions say to use an H-8 / 5 mm hook, then working the beginning chain with a J-9 / 5.5 mm hook will provide an edge that doesn't pucker, an important factor for the finished piece.

In the same vein, finish by working the final or last two rows or rounds with a US size or half size millimeter smaller hook. Sometimes crochet work draws in a bit but you don't want that to happen on the last rows/rounds. If you worked the piece with an H-8 / 5 mm hook, then finishing with a US 7 / 4.5 mm will insure that the edge will not be looser than the piece as a whole.

Tips: When you begin a piece with a lot of chain stitches, it's not always easy to keep count of the number of chains. To insure that you have enough chains, make a few extra. You can undo any extra chains after you've worked the first row. Make sure that the knot at the beginning of the chain is not too tight. When there are extra chain sts, pick out the knot and then use a hook to undo the extra chain stitches. When you are even with the end of the first row, pull yarn tail firmly through loop.

Crocheting in Rows
When you get to the end of the first row across, turn the work. You can turn clockwise or counterclockwise. Decide how you want to turn and then work the same way throughout the piece. At the beginning of the next row, make the correct number of chain sts (ch) to substitute for the first st (sc, dc, hdc, dc, tr, etc). Make 1 ch for a sc, 2 for a hdc, 3 for a dc, 4 for tr, and 5 for dbl tr.

Crocheting in the Round
Instead of crocheting back and forth in rows, you can work in the round. Begin with the number of chain stitches specified in the instructions and then join the ring with a slip stitch into the first ch. If you are going to make a flat disk, make sure that the increases are evenly spaced around throughout. If you are making a tube, crochet around and around without increasing. Each round begins with the same number of chain sts appropriate for the stitch (see Crocheting in Rows). End each round with a slip st into the first st of the round.

Differentiating Rows and Round in a Pattern
When you crochet back and forth, you are working in *rows*. When you crochet around, you are working in *rounds*.

Once you know if a piece is worked in rows or rounds, then you will understand how the piece is constructed. Sometimes both methods are used in one piece. For example, you might be crocheting netting for a bag in the round but then you crochet the handles back and forth.

Joining Yarn and Changing Colors
It is best to change or join yarn at the side of a piece or at the beginning of a round but sometimes that isn't possible. In that case, catch one yarn tail with the stitches as you crochet and catch the other yarn end on the next round or row. Tails can also be woven in during finishing by threading into the backs of stitches with a tapestry needle.

Usually colors are changed at the beginning of a round or at the side. For a smooth transition between the colors, work as follows: before you begin the last stitch prior to the color change, make sure that the yarn to be dropped is on the wrong side of the piece. Crochet to the last yarnover on the stitch with the old color, yarn over hook with the new color and pull new color through on the last step of the stitch. Now continue with the new color. In this way, each of the stitches will each be worked with its own color.

Crochet Gauge
Each pattern specifies the gauge and you should make a swatch to test the gauge. Crochet a swatch about 6 x 6 in / 15 x 15 cm and take measurements within the center 4 x 4 in / 10 x 10 cm. Count the number of stitches and rows. It is important to make a gauge swatch bigger than 4 x 4 in / 10 x 10 cm because it will pull in a bit at the outer edges. If the stitch count doesn't match that in the pattern, change to a larger or smaller size hook. If there are too many stitches change to a larger hook and if there are too few stitches use a smaller hook.

Buy Enough Yarn (Yarn suppliers on page 90)
It is important to have enough yarn on hand before you start a piece. If you've already begun and have to buy more yarn, you may not be able to get the same dyelot and the colors won't match.
I also recommended that you always use good quality yarn to ensure the best results and the most enjoyable crocheting. The process is as important as the finished result!

Dishrags

Each dishcloth is made with a different type of stitch—single crochet, half double, double, treble and some in the back loops on the stitch. Each yields a different structure, firmness and elasticity.

Single crochet makes a firm and close structure, but, if you work in the back loops only, the texture is softer and looks like ribbed crochet.

Half double crochet makes a somewhat softer and less firm surface with a more rib-like effect.

Double crochet produces an even softer and more open structure. The structure looks different but not rib-like if you crochet into the back loops only.

Treble crochet makes the softest and most open structure. Crochet into the back loops for a non-ribbed and different effect.

Single crochet

Single crochet into back loops

Half Double crochet

Half Double crochet into back loops

Double crochet

Treble crochet

Materials:
Yarn: DK (CYCA #3)
Shown here: Du Store
Alpakka, T'ika (100% Pima
cotton), 150 g yellow T504
Substitution: Mirasol T'ika
#504 (100% Pima cotton)
91 yds / 83 m / 50 g
Crochet hook:
US 7 / 4.5 mm

Measurements: approx
13 x 13 in / 32.5 x 32.5 cm

Yellow dishrag
in single crochet

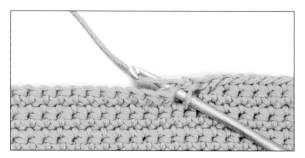

Step 1: *Insert hook through both loops on top of stitch, yarn around hook.*

Instructions:

Chain 53.

Row 1: Beg in 2nd ch from hook, work 52 sc into chain; turn.

Row 2: Ch 1 (= 1 sc), work 1 sc into each sc across; turn.

Row 3: As for Row 2.

Repeat Row 2 until piece is about 12 in / 30.5 cm long or squared.

Edging:

Round 1: Beg in a corner, ch 1 and 2 sc into corner st.

Side 1 (top of piece): 1 sc into each sc across; 3 sc into next corner.

Side 2 (side of piece): 1 sc into each sc row; 3 sc into corner.

Side 3 (lower edge): 1 sc into each chain (beg chain); 3 sc into corner.

Side 4: As for Side 2, ending with 1 sl st into 1st ch.

Round 2: Work 1 crab st into each sc around, ending with 1 sl st into 1st crab st (see page 24).

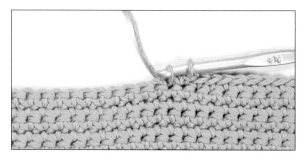

Step 2: *Pull the yarn through both stitch loops.*

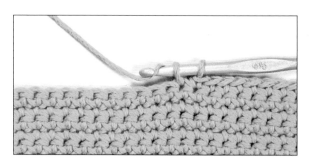

Step 3: *Yarn around hook and through both loops on the hook.*

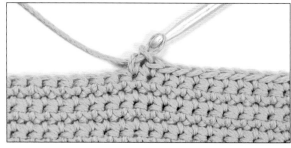

Step 4: *When there is only one loop on the hook and 1 completed sc, repeat steps 1-3 for each single crochet.*

Note: *Slip stitches are made as for single crochet but, in step 2, the yarn is pulled through the stitch and the loops on the hook at the same time. Slip stitches are used to join the end to the beginning of a round. If you don't join with a slip st, eventually you won't be able to see where the round begins.*

Materials:
Yarn: DK (CYCA #3)
Shown here: Du Store
Alpakka, T'ika (100% Pima
cotton), 100 g orange T503
Substitution: Mirasol T'ika
#503 (100% Pima cotton)
91 yds / 83 m / 50 g
Crochet hook:
US 7 / 4.5 mm

Measurements: approx
11¾ x 11¾ in / 30 x 30 cm

14

Orange dishrag
in single crochet through back loops

Step 1: Insert hook through the back loop of stitch, yarn around hook.

Instructions:

Chain 53.

Row 1: Beg in 2nd ch from hook, work 52 sc into chain; turn.

Row 2: Ch 1 (= 1 sc), work 1 sc into back loop of each sc across; turn.

Row 3: As for Row 2.

Note: On the last sc of each row, work through both loops.

Repeat Row 2 until piece is about 11¾ in / 30 cm long or squared. Crocheting into back loops only makes the fabric pull in length- and width-wise. Do not stretch the piece when measuring.

This dishrag doesn't have an edging so the elasticity won't be affected.

Step 2: Pull the yarn through the back loop of the stitch.

Step 3: Yarn around hook and through both loops on the hook.

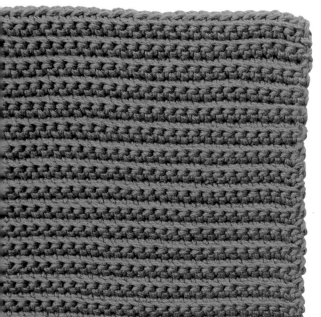

Step 4: When there is only one loop on the hook and 1 completed sc, repeat steps 1-3 for each single crochet. Working into the back loops only produces a ribbed effect and a very elastic fabric.

Materials:
Yarn: DK (CYCA #3)
Shown here: Du Store Alpakka, T'ika (100% Pima cotton), 150 g red T509
Substitution: Mirasol T'ika #509 (100% Pima cotton) 91 yds / 83 m / 50 g
Crochet hook:
US 7 / 4.5 mm

Measurements: approx 14¼ x 14¼ in / 36 x 36 cm

Red dishrag
in half double crochet

Step 1: Yarn round hook and insert hook through both loops on top of stitch, yarn around hook.

Instructions:
Chain 54.
Row 1: Beg in 3rd ch from hook, work 52 hdc into chain; turn.
Row 2: Ch 2 (= 1 hdc), work 1 hdc into each hdc across; turn.
Row 3: As for Row 2.
Repeat Row 2 until piece is about 13 in / 33 cm long or squared.

Edging:
Round 1: Beg in a corner and ch 1 and 2 sc in corner stitch.
Side 1 (top): 1 sc into each hdc across, 3 sc into next corner.
Side 2 (side): 1 sc in about every hdc row, 3 sc in corner.
Side 3 (lower edge): 1 sc in each chain (beg ch), 3 sc in corner.
Side 4: As for Side 2, ending rnd with 1 sl st into 1st st.
Round 2: Ch 1, *1 sc into sc, ch 3, 1 sl st into last sc (= picot), 1 sc into sc*; repeat * to * around, ending with 1 sl st into ch.

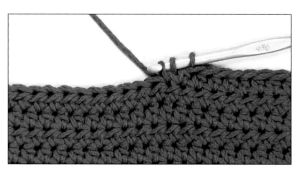

Step 2: Pull the yarn through both stitch loops.

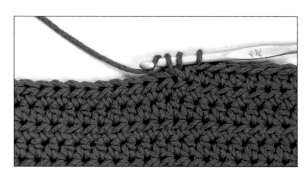

Step 3: Yarn around hook and through all 3 loops on the hook.

Step 4: When there is only one loop on the hook and 1 completed hdc, repeat steps 1-3 for each half double crochet.

Materials:
Yarn: DK (CYCA #3)
Shown here: Du Store Alpakka, T'ika (100% Pima cotton), 100 g purple T531
Substitution: Mirasol T'ika (100% Pima cotton)
91 yds / 83 m / 50 g
Crochet hook:
US 7 / 4.5 mm

Measurements: approx 12¼ x 12¼ in / 31 x 31 cm

Purple dishrag
in half double crochet through back loops

Instructions:
Chain 54.
Row 1: Beg in 3rd ch from hook, work 52 hdc into chain; turn.
Row 2: Ch 2 (= 1 hdc), work 1 hdc into back loop of each hdc across; turn.
Row 3: As for Row 2.
Repeat Row 2 until piece is about 11¾ in / 30 cm long or squared.

Edging:
Round 1: Beg in a corner and make ch 1 and 2 sc in corner stitch.
Side 1 (top): 1 sc into each hdc across, 3 sc into next corner.
Side 2 (side): 1 sc in about every hdc row, 3 sc in corner.
Side 3 (lower edge): 1 sc in each chain (beg ch), 3 sc in corner.
Side 4: As for Side 2, ending rnd with 1 sl st into 1st st.
Round 2: Ch 1, 3 sc in corner *1 sc into sc across, 3 sc in corner *; rep * to * around, ending round with 1 sl st into ch.

Half Double Crochet through Back Loops

Step 1: Yarn round hook and insert hook through back loop of stitch, yarn around hook.

Step 2: Pull the yarn through back loop of stitch.

Step 3: Yarn around hook and through all 3 loops on the hook.

Step 4: When there is only one loop on the hook and 1 completed hdc, repeat steps 1-3 for each half double crochet through back loop. Working half double crochet through the back loops only produces a very elastic ribbed fabric, although single crochet through back loops makes a more elastic fabric.

Materials:
Yarn: DK (CYCA #3)
Shown here: Du Store
Alpakka, T'ika (100% Pima
cotton), 150 g purple T510
Substitution: Mirasol T'ika
#510 (100% Pima cotton)
91 yds / 83 m / 50 g
Crochet hook:
US 7 / 4.5 mm

Measurements: approx.
14½ x 14½ in / 37 x 37 cm

Dark purple
dishrag in double crochet

Double Crochet (dc)

Step 1: Yarn round hook and insert hook through both loops at top of stitch, yarn around hook.

Instructions:

Chain 55.

Row 1: Beg in 4th ch from hook, work 52 dc into chain; turn.

Row 2: Ch 3 (= 1 dc), work 1 dc into each dc across; turn.

Row 3: As for Row 2.

Repeat Row 2 until piece is about 13½ in / 34 cm long or squared.

Edging:

Round 1: Beg in a corner and make ch 1 and 2 sc in corner stitch.

Side 1 (top): 1 sc into each dc across, 3 sc into next corner.

Side 2 (side): 1 sc in about every dc row, 3 sc in corner.

Side 3 (lower edge): 1 sc in each chain (beg ch), 3 sc in corner.

Side 4: As for Side 2, ending rnd with 1 sl st into 1st st.

Round 2: 7 dc in corner *skip 1 sc, 5 dc in next sc (= fan), skip 1 sc, 1 sc in next sc*; rep from * to * to next corner, 7 dc in corner sc; rep from * to * along next 3 sides and end with sl st to 1st dc at corner.

Step 2: Pull the yarn through both stitch loops.

Step 3: Yarn around hook (there are now 3 loops on hook), pull yarn through the first 2 loops on hook (2 loops now remain on hook). Yarn around hook and through both loops on hook.

Step 4: When there is only one loop on the hook and 1 completed dc, repeat steps 1-3 for each double crochet.

Materials:
Yarn: DK (CYCA #3)
Shown here: Du Store Alpakka, T'ika (100% Pima cotton), 150 g royal blue T507
Substitution: Mirasol T'ika #507 (100% Pima cotton) 91 yds / 83 m / 50 g
Crochet hook:
US 7 / 4.5 mm

Measurements: approx 15 x 15 in / 38 x 38 cm

Blue dishrag
in treble crochet

Treble Crochet (tr)

Step 1: Yarn round hook twice and insert hook through both loops at top of stitch, yarn around hook. Pull the yarn through both stitch loops (there are now 4 loops on hook).

Step 2: Yarn around hook and pull yarn through the first 2 loops on hook (3 loops now remain on hook).

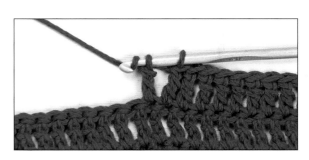

Step 3: Yarn around hook and through two loops on hook (2 loops remain on hook).

Step 4: Yarn around hook; pull yarn through rem 2 loops on hook. When there is only one loop on the hook and 1 completed tr, repeat steps 1-3 for each treble crochet.
Note: A double treble (dbl tr) is worked the same way but begun with yarn around the hook 3 times; a triple treble begins with yarn around the hook 4 times.

Instructions:
Chain 56.
Row 1: Beg in 5th ch from hook, work 52 tr into chain; turn.
Row 2: Ch 4 (= 1 tr), work 1 tr into each tr across; turn.
Row 3: As for Row 2.
Repeat Row 2 until piece is about 13½ in / 34 cm long or squared.

Edging:
Round 1: Beg in a corner and make ch 1 and 2 sc in corner stitch.
Side 1 (top): 1 sc into each dc across, 3 sc into next corner.
Side 2 (side): 1 sc in about every tr row, 3 sc in corner.
Side 3 (lower edge): 1 sc in each chain (beg ch), 3 sc in corner.
Side 4: As for Side 2, ending rnd with 1 sl st into 1st st.
Round 2: Ch 1, *1 sc in next sc, ch 5, 1 sl st into last sc, 1 sc in next sc, ch 7, 1 sl st in last sc, 1 sc in next sc, ch 5, 1 sl st in last sc, (1 sc in next sc) 2 times*; rep from * to *around, ending with 1 sl st into first ch.

Crab stitch (worked from left to right)

This stitch is used most often as a finishing or edging and is crocheted from left to right, giving the stitch an extra "twist."

Step 1: *Do not turn work after last row. After completing last row, insert hook through both loops of the first stitch to the right, turn hook so that you can pick up the yarn and bring yarn around hook.*

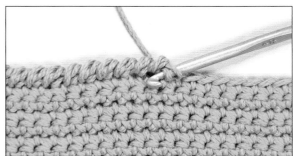

Step 2: *Pull yarn through the stitch.*

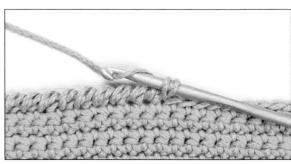

Step 3: *Yarn around hook and pull through both loops on hook.*

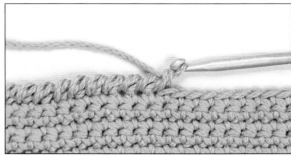

Step 4: *When only 1 loop remains on hook and the crab stitch has been completed, repeat Steps 1-3 for each crab stitch.*

Lap afghan

Gather all the leftover yarns in your stash to make this granny square afghan for a little one.
Tip: Use the yarn you have least of for the center of the blocks and save the larger amounts for the longer rounds.

Materials:
Yarn: Sport (CYCA #2)
Shown here: Garnstudio Drops Alpaca (100% alpaca) 5 ply, 182 yds / 167 m, 50 g, 50 g each of 7240 petrol mix, 6205 light blue, 2919 teal/dark turquoise, 7238 dark olive mix, 7815 petrol/green mix, 3140 light pink, 618 dark beige, 4050 purple, 7300 lime, 7233 olive mix, 6790 dark slate blue, 4400 dark purple, 2921 raspberry pink, 2923 goldenrod yellow, 7120 light gray green, 3650 maroon mix, 2922 deep pinkish red, 2110 wheat, 501 light gray, 8903 black, 100 off-white; 100 g 100 off-white, 3620 red
Hook: US E-4 / 3.5 mm

Instructions:

One Block

Ch 6 and join into a ring with sl st.

Round 1: Ch 6 (= 1 dc + 3 ch), (3 dc into ring, ch 3) 3 times, 2 dc into ring and end with sl st into 3rd ch of ch-6 at beg of round.

Round 2: Sl st to center of the first dc group, ch 6 (= 1 dc + 3 ch), 3-dc gr into same loop, *ch 1, (3-dc gr, ch 3, 3-dc gr) around next ch loop*; rep to * twice; ch 1, 2 dc around same ch loop as beg with 6 ch and end round with 1 sl st into 3rd ch of the ch 6 at beg of rnd.

Round 3: Sl st to center of 1st ch loop, ch 6 (= 1 dc + 3 ch), 3-dc gr around same loop, *ch 1, 3-dc gr around next loop, ch 1, * * [3-dc gr, ch 3, 3-dc gr] in next loop; rep from * 2 times and * to * * 1 time; 2 dc in same ch as beg with ch 6 and end rnd with 1 sl st into 3rd ch of the ch 6 at beg of rnd.

Round 4: Sl st to center of 1st ch loop, ch 6 (= 1 dc + 3 ch), 3-dc gr around same loop, *ch 1, [3-dc gr in next loop, ch 1] 2 times, **[3-dc gr, ch 3, 3-dc gr] in next loop; rep from * 2 times and from ** 1 time; 2 dc in same loop as beg with ch 6 and end rnd with 1 sl st into 3rd ch of the ch 6 at beg of rnd. Cut yarn.

Round 5: Change to a new color. Begin in a corner loop with 6 ch (= 1 dc + 3 ch), 3-dc group around same loop, *ch 1, [3 dc in next loop, ch 1] 3 times, **[3-dc group, ch 3, 3-dc group] in next loop; rep from * 2 times and from * to * * 1 time, 2 dc in same ch as beg with ch 6 and end rnd with 1 sl st into 3rd ch of the ch 6 at beg of rnd.

Round 6: Sl st to center of 1st ch loop, ch 6 (= 1 dc + 3 ch), 3-dc gr around same loop, *ch 1, [3-dc gr in next loop, ch 1] 4 times, ** [3-dc gr, ch 3, 3-dc gr] in next

loop; rep from * 2 times and from * to * * 1 time; 2 dc in same loop as beg with ch 6 and end rnd with 1 sl st into 3rd ch of the ch 6 at beg of rnd. Cut yarn.

Round 7: Change to a new color. Begin in a corner loop with 6 ch (= 1 dc + 3 ch), 3-dc group around same loop, *ch 1, [3 dc in next loop, ch 1] 5 times, **[3-dc group, ch 3, 3-dc group] in next loop; rep from * 2 times and from * to * * 1 time, 2 dc in same ch as beg with ch 6 and end rnd with 1 sl st into 3rd ch of the ch 6 at beg of rnd.

Round 8: Sl st to center of 1st ch loop, ch 6 (= 1 dc + 3 ch), 3-dc gr around same loop, *ch 1, [3-dc gr in next loop, ch 1] 6 times, ** [3-dc gr, ch 3, 3-dc gr] in next loop; rep from * 2 times and from ** 1 time; 2 dc in same loop as beg with ch 6 and end rnd with 1 sl st into 3rd ch of the ch 6 at beg of rnd. Cut yarn.

Round 9: Change color. Work as for Round 7 but add 1 3-dc group (3 dc in loop) and 1 ch on each side of the block.

Round 10: Work as for Round 8 but add 1 3-dc group (in loop) and 1 ch on each side of the block.

Round 11: Change color. Work as for Round 7 but add 1 3-dc group (in loop) and 1 ch on each side of the block.

Round 12: Work as for Round 8 but add 1 3-dc group (in loop) and 1 ch on each side of the block. Cut yarn.

Round 13: Change color. Work as for Round 7 but add 1 3-dc group (in loop) and 1 ch on each side of the block.

Round 14: Work as for Round 8 but add 1 3-dc group (in loop) and 1 ch on each side of the block. Cut yarn.
Weave in all yarn tails neatly on WS.

Make a total of 24 blocks in various color combinations.

Finishing:

With WS facing, crochet the blocks together as follows: Place blocks 1 and 2 next to each other (see diagram, RS faces RS) and begin crocheting at one corner with 1 sc through the ch loops of both blocks. * ch 1, skip 1 ch, 1 sl st in dc through both blocks, ch 1, skip 1 dc, 1 sl st in dc through both blocks*; rep from * to * to the corner. At the corner, work 1 sc through the ch loop of both blocks (do not cut yarn). Place block 3 edge to edge on the next side of block 1, RS facing RS and continue to work 1 sc through ch loops of both blocks, * ch 1, skip 1 ch, 1 sl st in dc through both blocks, 1 ch, skip 1 dc, 1 sl st in dc through block *; rep * to * to the corner. At the corner work 1 sc through ch loop of both blocks; cut yarn and weave in ends on WS. Continue joining, with blocks 4, 5, and 6 crocheted to blocks 2 and 3 (see diagram). Join the blocks diagonally. See diagram for the sequence of joining blocks.

Crocheted Edging:

Round 1: With light blue, begin at a corner chain with

6 ch (= 1 dc + 3 ch), 3 dc in same loop, * ch 1, 3 dc in next loop (= 1 dc-group)*; rep from * to * to corner (at the join between two blocks, work 1 dc-group), ** 3 dc, ch 3, 3 dc** in next loop/corner; rep from * to * on each long side and from ** to ** at each corner. End round with 1 sl st into 3rd ch of the ch 6 at beg of round. Cut yarn.

Round 2: Change to red and begin at a corner chain loop with 6 ch (= 1 dc + 3 ch), 3 dc in same loop, * ch 1, 3 dc in next ch (- 1 dc group)*; rep from * to * to corner, **3 dc, ch 3, 3 dc** in next loop/corner; rep from * to * on each long side and from ** to ** at each corner. End round with 1 sl st into 3rd ch of the ch 6 at beg of round.

Round 3: Sl st to center of 1st loop, ch 6 (= 1 dc + ch 3), 3 dc in same loop, * ch 1, 3 dc in next loop (= 1 dc group)*; rep from * to * to corner, ** 3 dc, ch 3, 3 dc** in next loop/corner; rep from * to * on each long side and from ** to ** at each corner. End round with 1 sl st into 3rd ch of the ch 6 at beg of round. Cut yarn.

Round 4: Change to off-white and work as for Round 2.

Round 5: Work as for Round 3.

Round 6: Change to red and work as for Round 2.

Round 7: Work as for Round 3; cut yarn.

Round 8: Ch 1, 1 sc in each st around and end round with 1 sl st into 1st sc. Cut yarn.

Weave in all yarn tails neatly on WS. Carefully steam press afghan.

Joining the blocks of the afghan

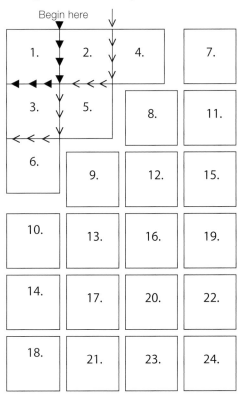

Measurements:
9 x 76¾ in / 23 x 195 cm

Pink and white scarf

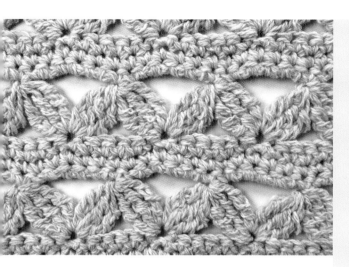

Instructions:

Holding one strand each white and pink together, ch 182.
Row 1: 1 sc in 2nd chain from hook, 1 sc in each chain across = 181 sc; turn.
Row 2: Ch 1, 1 sc in each sc across; turn.
Row 3: Ch 5 (= 1 dbl tr), skip 2 sc, 3-dbl tr cluster (see above) into sc, ch 5, paired 3-dbl tr cluster (see above), *ch 5, paired 3-dbl tr cluster (first half of the paired 3-dbl tr cluster is worked in the same sc as the previous cluster, see photo)*; rep * to * across until 3 sc remain. End with ch 5, 3-dbl tr cluster in same sc as previous cluster but do not pull the yarn through the last time, skip 2 sc, 1 dbl tr in last sc and pull yarn through 4 dbl tr all at once (the last dbl tr and 3-dbl tr cluster), turn.
Row 4: Ch 1, 1 sc in top of the 3-dbl tr cluster, 5 sc over the ch 5 loops *1 sc in top of the paired 3-dbl tr cluster, 5 sc around ch 5 loop*; rep * to * and end with 1 sc in top of the 3-dbl tr cluster; turn.
Row 5: Ch 1, 1 sc in each sc across; turn.
Row 6: Ch 1, 1 sc in each sc across; turn.
Repeat Rows 3-6 throughout – these 4 rows are the pattern repeat. Work the pattern repeat a total of 3 times.

Edging:

1st row along short side only: *1 sc in each row of sc, 5 sc over a dbl tr or ch-5 loop*; rep * to * across short edge of scarf; turn.
2nd row along short side only: Ch 1, 1 sc in each sc across; cut yarn.
Edge the other short side of the scarf the same way.
finish by working 1 sc into each sc across each side and 3 sc into each corner.
Cut yarn and weave in ends on WS. Lightly steam press scarf to block.

Materials:

Yarn: Worsted (CYCA #4)
Shown here: Garnstudio Drops Angora-Tweed (30% angora/70% Merino wool) 158 yds / 145 m, 50 g, 200 g each natural white 10 and pink 14
Substitutions: Garnstudio Drops Lima (65% wool/35% alpaca) 98 yds / 90 m, 50 g Garnstudio Drops Merino Extra Fine (100% Merino wool superwash) 115 yds / 105 m, 50 g
Hook: US M/N13 / 9 mm
Gauge: 10 sc with doubled yarn and hook US M/N / 9 mm = 4 in / 10 cm.

The scarf is crocheted with one strand of each color held together.

Double Treble Cluster (dbl tr cluster): the number of double trebles to make for each cluster is indicated by the number before the abbreviation for the cluster, for example 3-dbl tr cluster.
Paired Double Treble Cluster (paired dbl tr cluster): the number of double trebles to make for each cluster is indicated by the number before the cluster abbreviation. For example, paired 3-dbl tr cluster. Work as for a dbl tr cluster to the last step when 3 loops remain on the hook, skip 5 sc and make another 3-dbl tr cluster and then finish with yarn around hook and through all 6 loops on the hook to make 1 stitch from the paired clusters.
Pattern repeat = 6 stitches.

Child's scarf

Materials:

Yarn: Worsted (CYCA #4)

Shown here: Garnstudio Drops Angora-Tweed (30% angora/70% Merino wool) 158 yds / 145 m, 50 g, 150 g each natural white 10 and pink 14

Substitutions: Garnstudio Drops Lima (65% wool/35% alpaca) 98 yds / 90 m, 50 g Garnstudio Drops Merino Extra Fine (100% Merino wool superwash) 115 yds / 105 m, 50 g

Hook: US J-9 / 5.5 mm

Gauge: 14 sc with doubled yarn and hook USJ- 9 / 5.5 mm = 4 in / 10 cm

Double Treble Cluster (dbl tr cluster): the number of double trebles to make for each cluster is indicated by the number before the abbreviation for the cluster, for example 3-dbl tr cluster.

Paired Double Treble Cluster (paired dbl tr cluster): the number of double trebles to make for each cluster is indicated by the number before the cluster abbreviation. For example, paired 3-dbl tr cluster. Work as for a dbl tr cluster to the last step when 3 loops remain on the hook, skip 5 sc and make a 3-dbl tr cluster and then finish with yarn around hook and through all 6 loops on the hook to make 1 stitch from the paired clusters.

Pattern repeat = 6 stitches.

Measurements: 7½ x 63¾ in / 19 x 162 cm including fringe

Instructions:

Ch 26.

Row 1: 1 sc in 2nd ch from hook, 1 sc in each ch across = 25 sc; turn.

Row 2: Ch 1, 1 sc in each sc across; turn.

Row 3: Ch 1, 1 sc in each sc across; turn.

Row 4: Ch 5 (= 1 dbl tr), skip 2 sc, 3-dbl tr cluster (see above) into sc, ch 5, paired 3-dbl tr cluster (see above), *ch 5, paired 3-dbl tr cluster (the first half of the paired 3-dbl tr cluster is worked into the same sc as the previous paired 3-dbl tr cluster (see photo)*; repeat * to *across until 3 sc remain. End with ch 5, 3-dbl tr cluster into same sc as previous paired 3-dbl tr cluster but end before last step of forming stitch, skip 2 sc, 1 dbl tr in the last sc and then pull the yarn through 4 dbl tr at the same time (the last dbl tr and the 3-dbl tr cluster); turn.

Row 5: Ch 1, 1 sc in top of 3-dbl tr cluster, 5 sc over ch 5 loop, *1 sc in top of paired 3-dbl tr cluster, 5 sc over ch 5 loop*; rep * to * across, ending with 1 sc in top of 3-dbl tr cluster; turn.

Row 6: Ch 1, 1 sc in each sc across; turn.

Row 7: Ch 1, 1 sc in each sc across; turn.

Repeat Rows 4-7 throughout – these 4 rows = pattern repeat. Work a total of 30 pattern repeats.

Edging:

Round 1 (long side): Ch 1, *1 sc in each row of sc, 5 sc over each dbl tr*; rep * to * along long side, work 3 sc in corner. Along the short side, work 1 sc into each sc of the first sc row; rep * to * on the next long side, 3 sc in corner, and 1 sc into each sc of short side, and end the round with 1 sl st into first ch.

Round 2: On the long side, sc into each sc. On the short end, make the fringe: *1 sc into sc, ch 10 and, beginning in 2nd ch from hook, work back with 1 sc into each ch = 9 sc, 1 sc into next sc on short side*; rep * to * along short end, finishing with 1 sc. Work sc into each sc on other long side and then work * to * on other short side. Cut yarn and weave in tail neatly on WS. Lightly steam press to block.

Striped baby hats

Materials:

Yarn: Sport (CYCA #2)

Shown here: Du Store Alpakka, Babysilk [TM1]
(80% baby alpaca/20% silk) 145 yds / 133 m, 50 g

Striped pink and white hat

50 g each natural white 301 and pink 312

Striped light blue and beige hat

50 g each light blue 313 and beige 324

Substitution: Diamond Yarn: Luxury Collection Baby
Silk (80% baby alpaca/20% silk) 145 yds / 133 m,
50 g (Sport, 5 ply)

Hook: US E-4 / 3.5 mm

Instructions:

Striped pink and white hat

With white, ch 4 and join into a ring with sl st.

Round 1: Ch 2 (= 1 hdc), 11 hdc into ring; end with 1 sl st into 2nd ch.

Round 2: Change to pink, ch 2 (= 1 hdc), 1 hdc in the same ch, 2 hdc in each hdc around and end with 1 sl st into 2nd ch = 24 hdc around.

Round 3: Change to white, ch 2, 1 hdc in same ch, 1 hdc in next hdc, *2 hdc in next st, 1 hdc in next st*; rep from * to * around, and end with 1 sl st into 2nd ch = 36 hdc.

Round 4: Change to pink, ch 2, 1 hdc in same ch, 1 hdc in next 2 hdc, *2 hdc in next hdc, 1 hdc into next 2 hdc*; rep * to * around, and end with 1 sl st into 2nd ch = 48 hdc.

Round 5: Change to white and repeat Rnd 4 with 3 hdc between each increase = 60 hdc.

Round 6: Change to pink and repeat Rnd 4 with 4 hdc between each increase = 72 hdc.

Round 7: Change to white, ch 2, 1 hdc in each hdc around and end with 1 sl st into 2nd ch.

Round 8: Change to pink and repeat Rnd 7.

Round 9: Change to white and repeat Rnd 7.

Round 10: Change to pink and repeat Rnd 7.

Round 11: Change to white and repeat Rnd 7.

Round 12: Change to pink and repeat Rnd 7.

Round 13: Change to white and repeat Rnd 7.

Round 14: Change to pink and repeat Rnd 7.

Round 15: Change to white and repeat Rnd 7.

Round 16: Change to pink and repeat Rnd 7.

Round 17: Change to white and repeat Rnd 7.

Round 18: Ch 1, 1 sc in each hdc around, and end with 1 sl st in ch.

Round 19: Ch 1, 1 sc in each sc around and end with 1 sl st in ch.

Repeat Rnd 19 five more times.

Last round: Change to pink, ch 1, 1 crab st in each sc around and end with 1 sl st into 1st crab st. Cut yarn.

Finishing:

Weave in all tails on WS. Lightly steam press hat. Fold up the brim at sc rows. Twist cords about 8 in / 20 cm long and sew them securely to edge of upturned brim, about 2¾ in / 7 cm to each side of the back "seam".

The instructions for the Striped Hat with Earflaps are on page 35.

Measurements: approx 13½ in / 34 cm diameter,
length 5¼ in / 13 cm

Sideways hat for a newborn

Measurements: approx 13¾ in / 35 cm circumference, 6¼ in / 16 cm long

Materials:
Yarn: Sport (CYCA #2)
Shown here: Du Store Alpakka, Babysilk [TM1] (80% baby alpaca/20% silk) 145 yds / 133 m, 50 g, 50 g each
light blue 313
and natural white 301
Substitution:
Diamond Yarn:
Luxury Collection Baby Silk (80% baby alpaca/20% silk) 145 yds / 133 m, 50 g (Sport, 5 ply)
Hook: US D-3 / 3 mm

If you crochet this hat with wool yarn, it will be quite elastic and will grow with the child. If you want a hat with a larger circumference, make the piece longer or increase 2-4-6-8 sts in width so that the hat is longer.

Instructions:
With light blue yarn, ch 62.

Row 1: Sc 1 in 2nd ch from hook, *ch 1, skip 1 ch, 1 sc into ch*; rep * to * across; turn.

Row 2: Ch 1, 1 sc in next sc, *1 sc into ch, ch 1, skip 1 sc*; rep * to * across and end with 1 sc in ch, 1 sc in sc; turn.

Row 3: Ch 1, 1 sc in sc, *ch 1, skip 1 sc, 1 sc in ch*; rep * to * across and end with ch 1, 1 sc in sc; turn.

Row 4: Work as for Row 2.

Row 5: Change to white and repeat Row 3.

Row 6: Work as for Row 2.

Row 7: Change to light blue and work as for Row 3. Repeat Rows 2 and 3 throughout. At the same time, work stripe sequence: 4 rows light blue and 2 rows white. Work in pattern until piece measures about 13¾ in / 35 cm and finish with 2 rows white.

Finishing:
Seam the sides with slip sts or sew by hand. Thread elastic cord into the top of the hat and pull together and sew top. Fold a doubled brim of ¾ and 1¼ in / 2 and 3 cm. Twist cords about 8 in / 20 cm long and sew them securely inside the doubled brim, about 2¾ in / 7 cm to each side of the back seam.

Striped hat with earflaps

Work as for the pink and white baby hat through Rnd 16. Begin by chaining with light blue which is used instead of natural white; beige substitutes for pink. See instructions on page 32.

Round 17 (Earflaps): Count 8 hdc to the left of center back (= beg of rnd). Change to light blue and work 15 hdc; turn.

Round 18: Change to beige and work in hdc, decreasing at the beginning and end of row by working the first and last two sts together = 13 hdc; turn.

Row 19: Change to light blue and work hdc across, decreasing at beg and end of row as for Row 18 = 11 hdc; turn.

Row 20: Change to beige and work hdc across, decreasing at beg and end of row as for Row 18 = 9 hdc; turn.

Row 21: Change to light blue and work hdc across, decreasing at beg and end of row as for Row 18 = 7 hdc; turn.

Row 22: Change to beige and work hdc across, decreasing at beg and end of row as for Row 18 = 5 hdc; turn.

Row 23: Change to light blue and work hdc across, decreasing at beg and end of row as for Row 18 = 3 hdc; cut yarn.

Make an earflap on the other side of the cap the same way, counting out 8 sts to the right from the center back + 13 hdc and begin here for the earflap.

Finish by working 1 rnd sc with light blue along lower edge of cap: work 1 sc in each hdc and 1 sc in each row along earflap sides. Make sure that the sc edging doesn't pucker or ruffle.

Finishing:
Weave in all yarn tails neatly on WS and lightly steam press hat. Twist two cords about 8 in / 20 cm long and sew one securely to tip of each earflap.

Pink and white baby blanket

Materials:

Sport (CYCA #2)

Shown here: Garnstudio Drops Baby Merino (100% Merino wool superwash extra fine) 191 yds / 175 m, 50 g, 350 g light pink 05 and 250 g natural white 01

Hook: US G-6 / 4 mm

Gauge: 23 sc = 4 in / 10 cm

Pattern Repeat = 3 stitches

Instructions:

With pink, ch 150.

Row 1: 1 sc into 2nd ch from hook, 1 sc in each ch across = 149 sc; turn.

Row 2: Ch 3, *skip 2 sc, 1 dc in next sc, ch 1, 1 dc in 1st sc that was skipped (crossed dc)*; rep * to * and end with 1 dc in last sc; turn.

Row 3: Ch 1, *1 sc in dc, 1 sc in ch, 1 sc in dc*; rep * to * across; turn.

Row 4: Work as for Row 2.

Row 5: Work as for Row 3.

Repeat Rows 2 and 3 until piece is about 32¼ in / 82 cm long and end with Row 3.

Edging:

Round 1: With pink, begin with 3 sc in corner. Long side: *1 sc in sc row, 2 sc over 3-ch loop or dc*; rep * to * along long side, work 3 sc in corner. Short side: 1 sc in each sc across and then 3 sc in corner. Work * to * along other long side, 3 sc in corner, and then 1 sc in each sc across short side; end with 1 sl st into 1st sc.

Round 2: Change to white, 1 sc in each sc and 3 sc in each corner around, end with 1 sl st into 1st sc.

Round 3: Begin with 3 sc in corner *skip 2 sc, 1 dc in sc, ch 1, 1 dc in sc that was skipped (crossed dc)*; rep * to * along long side, 3 dc in corner, rep * to * along short side, 3 dc in corner; rep * to * along long side, 3 dc in corner, rep * to * along short side and end with 1 sl st into 1st dc; turn.

Round 4: Ch 1, *1 sc in dc, 1 sc in ch, 1 sc in dc*; rep * to * around, working 3 sc in each corner stitch. End with 1 sl st into 1st sc; turn.

Round 5: Work as for Rnd 2.

Round 6: Work as for Rnd 3.

Round 7: Work as for Rnd 2.

Round 8: Work as for Rnd 3.

Round 9: Ch 1, sc into each sc around and end with 1 sl st into 1st ch.

Round 10, Ruffle: Ch 3, 1 dc in the same st as ch, 2 dc in each sc around, end with 1 sl st into 3rd ch.

Round 11: Ch 4, 1 tr in each dc around and end with 1 sl st into 4th ch.

Round 12: Ch 1, 1 crab st into each tr around, ending with 1 sl st into 1st crab st. Cut yarn.

Weave in all tails neatly on WS and lightly steam press blanket to block.

Measurements:
30 x 37¾ in / 76 x 96 cm

Measurements: approx
29½ x 37½ in / 75 x 95 cm

Soft silk and
alpaca baby blanket

Each block uses four colors. Three of the colors are used in various sequences for the flowers and the fourth color is used to edge the block. Note: Dark blue is never used for the borders, only for the flowers (see photo). Crochet 31 blocks with natural white borders, 16 with light blue, and 16 blocks with beige (= total of 63 blocks in varying color arrangements).

Materials:
Yarn: Sport (CYCA #2)
Shown here: Du Store Alpakka, Babysilk [TM1] (80% baby alpaca/20% silk) 145 yds / 133 m, 50 g, 250 g natural white 301, 150 g beige 324, 200 g light blue 313, and 150 g blue 314
Substitution: Diamond Yarn: Luxury Collection Baby Silk (80% baby alpaca/20% silk) 145 yds / 133 m, 50 g (Sport, 5 ply)
Hook: US D-3 / 3 mm

Instructions

Begin with dark blue, for example, and ch 6; join into a ring with sl st.

Round 1: Ch 1, 16 sc around ring and join with 1 sl st into 1st sc. Cut yarn.

Round 2: Change to a new color, beige, for example. Ch 6 (= 1 dc + ch 3), skip 2 sc, *1 dc in next sc, ch 3, skip 1 sc *; rep * to * 7 times and end round with 1 sl st into 3rd ch of the 6 ch at beg of rnd.

Round 3: Ch 1, *1 sc, 1 hdc, 3 dc, 1 hdc, 1 sc around ch-3 loop *; rep * to * 7 times and end with 1 sl st into 1st sc (8 petals around). Cut yarn.

Round 4: Change to a new color, light blue, for example. Attach yarn between 2 sc, ch 1, 1 sc in same place, ch 6, *1 sc between the next 2 sc, ch 6 *; rep * to * 6 times and end round with sl st into 1st sc.

Round 5: Ch 1, *1 sc, 1 hdc, 5 dc, 1 hdc, 1 sc around ch-6 loop *; rep * to * 7 times and end with 1 sl st into 1st sc (8 petals around). Cut yarn.

Round 6: Change to border color (natural white, for example). Attach yarn in 2nd dc of a petal with ch 1 and 1 sc into same dc, ch 6, skip 2 dc, 1 sc into next dc, *ch 6, 1 dc into 2nd dc of next petal, ch 6, skip 2 dc, 1 sc into next dc *; rep * to * 7 times and end with sl st into 1st sc.

Round 7: Sl st over to 6-ch loop, ch 3 (= 1 dc), 3 dc, ch 4, 4 dc around 6-ch loop (= corner) *, ch 4, 1 sc into next ch-6 loop, [ch 6, 1 sc into next ch-6 loop], rep [-] 2 times, ch 4, **[4 dc, ch 4, 4 dc] around next ch-6 loop (= corner). Rep from *2 times and from *- ** 1 time and end with 1 sl st into 3rd ch.

Round 8: Ch 3 (= 1 dc), 1 dc into each of the next 3 dc, *[3 dc, ch 2, 3 dc] into ch-4 loop (corner), 1 dc into each of the next 4 dc, ch 1, 2 dc into ch-4 loop, [ch 1, 3 dc around ch-6 loop] 2 times, ch 1, 2 dc around ch-4 loop, ch 1, ** 1 dc into each of the next 4 dc, rep from *2 times and from * - ** 1 time and end with sl st into 3rd ch.

(in the space between 2 blocks, work 1 dc into loop). **3 dc, ch 3, 3 dc **in next loop/corner; rep * to * on each long side and from ** to ** at each corner and end round with 1 sl st into 3rd ch at beg of rnd. Cut yarn.

Round 2: Change to white and begin in chain loop at corner with ch 3 (= 1 dc), 2 dc in same loop, ch 3, 3 dc in same loop, *1 dc in dc*; rep * to * to next corner, **3 dc, ch 3, 3 dc** in corner/loop; rep * to * along each long side and ** to ** at each corner. End rnd with 1 sl st into 3rd ch at beg of rnd. Cut yarn.

Round 3: Change to beige and begin in chain loop at corner with ch 3 (= 1 dc), 2 dc around same loop, ch 3, 3 dc in same loop, * 1 sc in dc*; rep from * to * to corner, **3 sc, ch 3, 3 sc** in loop/corner; rep * to * along each long side and ** to ** at each corner. End rnd with 1 sl st into 3rd ch at beg of rnd. Cut yarn.

Round 4: Change to light blue. Begin in the chain loop at a corner with ch 3 (= 1 dc), 2 dc in same loop, ch 3, 3 dc in same loop, *1 dc into sc*; rep from * to * to corner, **3 dc, ch 3, 3 dc** in next loop/corner; rep from * to * on each long side and from ** to ** in each corner. End round with 1 sl st into 3rd ch at beg of rnd. Cut yarn.

Round 5: Work as for Rnd 4.

Round 6: Work 1 crab st in each dc around. Cut yarn. Weave in all yarn tails neatly on WS. Lightly steam press blanket.

Weave in all yarn tails neatly on WS.

Finishing

With natural white, crochet the blocks together from the WS: RS facing RS of blocks 1 and 2 (see diagram for sequence), begin joining at one corner with 1 sc through the ch loops of both blocks, *ch 1, skip 1 ch, 1 sl st into dc through both blocks, ch 1, skip 1 dc, 1 sl st into dc through both blocks *; rep * to * to corner. At corner, work 1 sc through ch-loops of both blocks (do not cut yarn). Place block 3 edge to edge on the next side of block 1, RS facing RS and continue by working 1 sc through ch-loops of both blocks. *1 sc, skip 1 ch, 1 sl st into dc through both blocks, ch 1, skip 1 dc, 1 sl st into dc of both blocks *; rep * to * to next corner and work 1 sc through ch-loops of both blocks. Cut yarn and weave in yarn tails on WS. Continue crocheting blocks together, with blocks 4, 5, and 6 joined to blocks 2 and 3 (see drawing). Join blocks in the sequence shown on the diagram until all are joined.

Crocheted Edging

Round 1: Beg with light blue into a corner ch-loop with ch 3 (= 1 dc), 2 dc around same ch-loop, ch 3, 3 dc in same ch-loop, *1 dc in dc*; rep * to * to next corner

Joining the blocks of the afghan

40

Hexagonal block afghan

Materials:
Yarn: Aran/Worsted (CYCA #4)
Shown here: Garnstudio Drops Silk Alpaca (20% silk/80% baby alpaca) 66 yds / 60 m, 50 g, 200 g each natural white 0100, bleached white 1101, pearl gray 4010, light turquoise 7120, medium pink 3720, pink 3140, gray 9015, dark beige 0205, purple 4301, 400 g old rose 4300, and 1150 g light beige 1340
Substitution: Garnstudio Drops Nepal (65% wool/35% alpaca) 82 yds / 75 m, 50 g
Hook: US I-9 / 5.5 mm
Gauge: 1 hexagon measures approx 5¼ x 5½ in / 13 x 14 cm

Measurements:
42¼ x 78¾ in / 107 x 200 cm

Instructions:

One block

Ch 4 and join into a ring with sl st.

Round 1: Ch 3 (= 1 dc), 11 dc around ring. End with 1 sl st into 3rd ch.

Round 2: Change color, 2-dc cluster (ch 3 [= 1 dc], 1 dc into same st), ch 2, *2-dc cluster into next dc, ch 2*; rep * to * around and end with 1 sl st into 3rd ch. Cut yarn.

Round 3: Change color, 3-dc group into ch-2 loop (ch 3 for 1st dc in group), ch 1, *3-dc group in ch-2 loop, ch 1 *; rep * to * around and end with 1 sl st into 3rd ch. Cut yarn.

Round 4: Change color, 1 sc (beg with ch 1 instead of sc) around ch-1 loop, ch 3, *1 sc around next ch-1 loop, ch 3 *; rep * to * around and end with 1 sl st into 1st ch.

Round 5: 1 sl st into ch-3 loop, *3-dc group (ch 3 for 1st dc of 3-dc group), ch 2, 3-dc group in same ch-3 loop, 3-dc group in next ch-3 loop *; rep * to * around and end with 1 sl st into 3rd ch. Cut yarn.

Round 6: Change color (light beige – all blocks end with round of light beige). *Ch 2 (= 1 hdc), ch 2, 1 hdc around ch-2 loop at corner, 1 hdc into each of next 9 dc *; rep * to * around and end with 1 sl st into 2nd ch. Cut yarn.

Make a total of 128 blocks in varying color combinations but always use light beige for Rnd 6.

Finishing:

Sew or crochet the blocks together: Complete the first block as instructed above. Join blocks clockwise. Work block 2 to the 2nd corner of Rnd 6, 1 hdc and, instead of ch 2 in the corner, crochet the blocks together with 1 sl st: insert hook through the ch-2 loop (corner) of the block at the side and pull through with 1 sl st, 1 hdc over ch-2 loop, 1 hdc each in next 4 dc; insert hook through 4th and 5th hdc on second block and pull through with 1 sl st, 1 hdc into next 3 dc, insert hook between 8th and 9th hdc of the 2nd block and pull through with 1 sl st, 1 hdc each in next 4 dc, 1 hdc in ch-2 loop, insert hook through ch-2 loop (corner) of block at the side and pull through with 1 sl st, 1 hdc in ch-2 loop. Continue as usual with Rnd 6 or join the next side. Keep working blocks and joining until piece is length specified above. When joining 2 rows of blocks, insert the hook through all 3 corner loops at the same time.

Join blocks as follows: 9 rows with 8 blocks in each and 8 rows with 7 blocks each. Finish by joining each of the rows of blocks.

Edging:

Round 1: Light beige, beg with 1 hdc into corner of long side, *ch 3 (= 1 dc), 1 dc in each of next 8 hdc, 3 dc into ch-2 loop (corner), 1 dc in each of next 11 hdc, 3 dc into ch-2 loop (corner), 1 dc in each of next 9 hdc, decrease in next corner by skipping 1 hdc, 1 dc into block join, skip 1 hdc, joining these 3 sts for a decrease (as a decrease is usually made), 1 dc into each of next 7 hdc (of next block), dec as before*; rep * to * along long side. Crochet the corner block as for beg of rnd. Work short sides as follows: *3 dc in ch-2 loop, 1 dc into each of next 9 hdc, dec at inner corner as before, 1 dc each into next 9 hdc*; rep * to * along short side. Continue the same way along opposite long and short sides. End rnd with 1 sl st into 3rd ch.

Round 2: Work this round with dc into dc and 3 dc at corners. Dec as before on inner corners. Cut yarn.

Round 3: Change to old rose and work round with sc into each dc and 2 sc at corners, decreasing as before at inner corners.

Round 4: Ch 1, 1 crab st into each sc (but skip 1 sc at each inner corner) around. End with 1 sl st into 1st crab st. Cut yarn.

Weave in all yarn tails neatly on WS. Lightly steam press to block.

Flower scarf

This scarf is crocheted with many colors of a fine baby alpaca yarn. The small flowers are joined as you crochet each one and the exciting color play is produced by combining two colors at a time in endless variations.

Measurements
approx 10¼ x 63 in / 26 x 160 cm

Materials:
Yarn: Lace weight
Shown here: Tekstilmakeriet, Venne Baby Alpaca 20/2 (100% baby alpaca) 10000 m/kg sold in 50 g balls, 547 yds / 500 m, 50 g each beige 0-9207, gray 0-9411, pink 0-03009, dark pink 0-3033, burgundy 0-4077, purple 0-4022, dark purple 0-4023, light purple 0-4031, ochre 0-5040
Substitutions: Misti Alpaca lace (2-ply, 100% baby alpaca) 437 yds, 50 g or Isager Alpaca 1 (100% baby alpaca) 437 yds, 50 g
Hook: US C-2 / 2.5 mm
The scarf is worked with doubled yarn: hold 1 strand of each color together.
Gauge: 1 flower = 1¼ x 1¼ in / 3 x 3 cm when finished

Instructions:
Row 1:
Flower 1:
Holding 2 strands (two different colors) together, ch 5 and join into a ring with 1 sl st.
Round 1: Work 9 sc loosely into ring. Join with 1 sl st into 1st sc. Cut yarn and weave in ends.
Round 2: Change to 2 new colors held together, cutting yarn to 47¼ in / 1.2 m lengths. Work 1 sc into 1st sc, *ch 6, 1 sc into next sc*; rep * to * 8 times. Join with 1 sl st into 1st sc. Cut yarns.
Note: It is important to weave in yarn tails as you work to avoid yarns tangling around each other.

Flower 2:
Using 2 colors held together, ch 5 and join into a ring with 1 sl st.
Round 1: Work 9 sc loosely into ring. Join with 1 sl st into 1st sc. Cut yarn and weave in ends.
Round 2: Change to 2 new colors held together, cutting yarn to 47¼ in / 1.2 m lengths. Work 1 sc into 1st sc, [ch 6, 1 sc into next sc] 6 times, *ch 6, remove hook from stitch and insert it from RS through the second chain loop on flower 1, insert hook into ch loop of flower 2 and pull the ch loops through the ch loop on flower 1. Continue with 1 sc in next sc*; rep * to * to first ch loop of flower 1; the flowers are now joined in two chain loops. Cut yarns.

Flower 3:
Using 2 colors held together, ch 5 and join into a ring with 1 sl st.
Round 1: Work 9 sc loosely into ring. Join with 1 sl st into 1st sc. Cut yarn and weave in ends.
Round 2: Change to 2 new colors held together, cutting yarn to 47¼ in / 1.2 m lengths. Work 1 sc into 1st sc, [ch 6, 1 sc into next sc] 6 times, *ch 6, remove hook from stitch and insert it from RS through 4th loop on flower 2, insert hook into st on flower 3 and pull loop through flower 2; continue with 1 sc in next sc*; rep * to * 1 time, through 3rd loop on flower 2. Cut yarns. The flowers are now joined in two chain loops.

Repeat flower 3 until there are 9 flowers in the row.

Row 2:
Flower 1:
Using 2 colors held together, ch 5 and join into a ring with 1 sl st.
Round 1: Work 9 sc loosely into ring. Join with 1 sl st into 1st sc. Cut yarn and weave in ends.
Round 2: Change to 2 new colors held together, cutting yarn to 47¼ in / 1.2 m lengths. Work 1 sc into 1st sc, [ch 6, 1 sc into next sc] 6 times, *ch 6, remove hook from stitch and insert it from RS into 4th loop on flower 1 on 1st row, insert hook into st on flower 2 and pull loop through loop on flower 1; continue with 1 sc in next

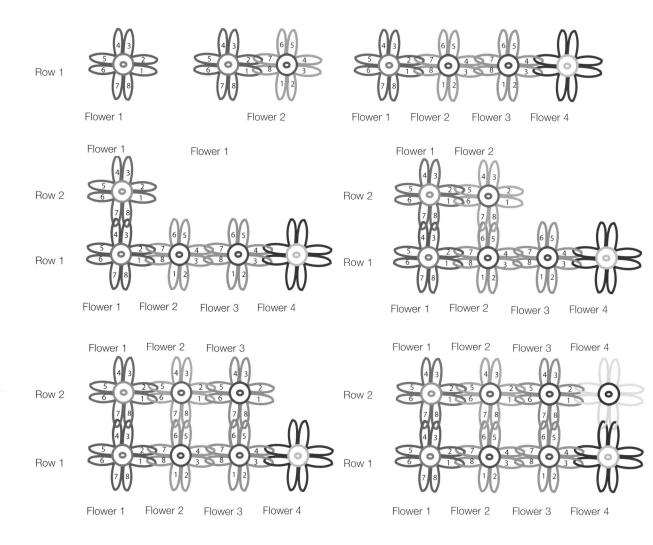

Row 1   Flower 1   Flower 2   Flower 1   Flower 2   Flower 3   Flower 4

Row 2   Flower 1   Flower 1

Row 1   Flower 1   Flower 2   Flower 3   Flower 4

Row 2   Flower 1   Flower 2

Row 1   Flower 1   Flower 2   Flower 3   Flower 4

Row 2   Flower 1   Flower 2   Flower 3   Flower 4

Row 1   Flower 1   Flower 2   Flower 3   Flower 4

Row 2   Flower 1   Flower 2   Flower 3   Flower 4

Row 1   Flower 1   Flower 2   Flower 3   Flower 4

sc*; rep * to * 1 time, through 3rd loop on flower 1 on 1st row. Cut yarns. The flowers are now joined in two chain loops.

Flower 2:
Using 2 colors held together, ch 5 and join into a ring with 1 sl st.
Round 1: Work 9 sc loosely into ring. Join with 1 sl st into 1st sc. Cut yarn and weave in ends.
Round 2: Change to 2 new colors held together, cutting yarn to 47¼ in / 1.2 m lengths. Work 1 sc into 1st sc, [ch 6, 1 sc into next sc] 4 times, *ch 6, remove hook from stitch and insert it from RS through 2nd loop of flower 1 on 2nd row; insert hook into st of flower 2 and pull loop through loop on flower 1; continue with 1 sc in next sc*; rep * to * 1 time through 1st loop of flower 1 of row 2; ch 6, remove hook from st and insert from RS through 6th loop of flower 2 on row 1, insert hook into st on flower and pull loop through loop on flower 2. Continue with 1 sc in next sc*; rep * to * 1 time through 5th loop of flower 2, row 1. Cut yarns. The flowers are now joined in 4 chain loops (2 loops from flower 1 of

Row 2 and 2 loops from flower 2, row 1). Repeat flower 2 until there 9 flowers in the row.

3rd and all following rows through row 65 or to desired length: Repeat Row 2.

Edging around scarf:
Beg on long side with 2 colors of yarn held together:
Round 1: *1 sc by inserting hook through both of the "loose" chain loops of a flower, ch 7*; rep * to * around, ending with 1 sl st into 1st sc.
Round 2: *1 sc in next sc, ch 1, 4 dc in 4th ch of loop (fan), ch 1*; rep * to * to corner. In each corner, work 7 dc into 4th ch of loop (fan); work * to *to next corner, work corner as before and continue around, ending with 1 sl st into 1st sc.

Finishing:
Pin scarf to finished measurements (approx 10¼ x 63 in / 26 x 160 cm) on a blocking board or mat (see detail photo on p. 47). Dampen scarf and leave until completely dry before removing pins.

Half gloves

Size: One Size

Materials:
Yarn: Lace weight
Shown here: Tekstilmakeriet, Venne Baby Alpaca 20/2 (100% baby alpaca) 10000 m/kg sold in 50 g balls, 547 yds / 500 m, color combination 1: 50 g each light blue 0-4060 and lilac 0-4022 OR combination 2: 50 g each pink 0-3009 and light lilac 0-4031
Substitutions: Misti Alpaca lace (2-ply, 100% baby alpaca) 437 yds, 50 g or Isager Alpaca 1 (100% baby alpaca) 437 yds, 50 g
Hook: US C-2 / 2.5 mm
Gauge: 38 dc in width and 19 rounds in length = 4 x 4 in / 10 x 10 cm
Pattern repeat = 3 sts

Right Half-Glove:
With 1 strand of each color held together, ch 60 a bit loosely; join into a ring with sl st.
Round 1: Ch 3, 1 dc into each ch and end rnd with 1 sl st into 3rd ch.
Round 2: Ch 3, *skip 1 dc, 1 dc into next dc, 1 dc into next dc, 1 dc in the dc that was skipped (st crosses over the previous two sts; these 3 sts = 1 pattern repeat)*; rep * to * around and end with 1 sl st into 3rd ch.
Rounds 3-23: Work as for Rnd 2.
Round 24: Work as for Rnd 2 until 4 repeats remain, ch 12 (skip the last 4 rep of rnd). End rnd with 1 sl st into 3rd ch. Thumbhole has just been made.
Round 25: Work as for Rnd 2 but work 4 repeats over the ch-12 loop.
Rounds 26-33: Work as for Rnd 2.
Round 34: Ch 1, 1 sc into each dc around and end with 1 sl st into ch.
Round 35: Work as for Rnd 34.
Round 36: Ch 1, *4 sc, skip 1 sc*; rep * to * around and end with 1 sl st into ch. Cut yarn.

Thumb:
Round 1: Begin at top of ch 3, attaching yarn with a sl st. Ch 3, *skip 1 ch, 1 dc into ch, 1 dc into ch, 1 crossed dc over to ch that was skipped*; rep * to * 2 times and then work crossed dc as before, 3 times, 2 dc in the 3 ch; end rnd with 1 sl st into 3rd ch.

Round 2: Work as for Rnd 2 of half glove. End rnd by decreasing the last 2 dc to 1 st and then work 1 sl st into 3rd ch.
Round 3: Work as for Rnd 2 of half glove. End rnd by skipping last dc and then work 1 sl st into 3rd ch.
Round 4: Work as for Rnd 2.
Round 5: Work as for Rnd 34.
Round 6: Work as for Rnd 34.
Round 7: Work as for Rnd 36.
Cut yarn.

Fan Edging:
Round 1: Attach yarn with 1 sl st into chain at beginning of half glove, ch 1 and then 1 sc into each ch around, ending with 1 sl st into 1st ch.
Round 2: *1 sc, skip 2 sc, 7 dc into next sc, skip 2 sc (= 1 fan)*; rep * to * around and end with 1 sl st into 1st sc. Cut yarn.

Left Half Glove:
Work as for Right Half Glove until Rnd 24.
Round 24: Ch 15 (skip over the first 4 repeats) and then continue as for Rnd 2, ending rnd with 1 sl st into 3rd ch. This forms the thumbhole.
The rest of the left half glove is worked as for the right hand glove.

Finishing:
Weave in all yarn tails neatly on WS and lightly steam press gloves under a pressing cloth.

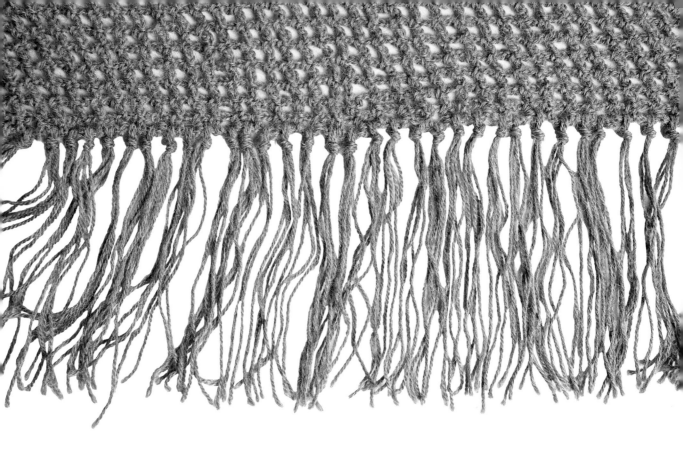

Crocheted shawl with chain stitch loops

Materials:
Yarn: Sport (CYCA #2)
Shown here: Garnstudio Alpaca (100% alpaca)
182 yds / 167 m, 50 g, six 50 g balls khaki/jeans
blue gray mix 8120
Hook: US D-3 – E4/3-3.5 mm; if you crochet
loosely, use the smaller size hook and the larger
hook if you crochet tightly

Instructions:
Ch 8, 1 tr into 1st ch; turn.
Row 1: Ch 8, 1 sc in ch loop, ch 3, 1 tr in same loop;
turn.
Row 2: Ch 8, 1 sc in loop, ch 5, 1 sc in next loop, ch 3,
1 tr in same loop; turn.
Row 3: Ch 8, 1 sc in loop, ch 5, 1 sc in next loop, ch 5,
1 sc in next loop, ch 3, 1 tr in same ch; turn.
Row 4: Ch 8, 1 sc in loop, ch 5, 1 sc in next loop, ch
5, 1 sc in next loop, ch 5, 1 sc in next loop, ch 3, 1 tr in
same loop; turn.
Row 5: Ch 8, 1 sc in loop, ch 5, 1 sc in next loop, ch 5,
1 sc in next loop, ch 5, 1 sc in next loop, ch 5, 1 sc in
next loop, ch 3, 1 tr in same loop; turn.
Continue the same way, increasing with 1 sc, ch 5 (= 1
chain loop) until there are 114-120 chain loops per row
or to desired size.
Knot fringe into the chain loops along each long edge.
Cut yarn into 11 in / 28 cm lengths and use 2 strands
for each fringe. Use a crochet hook to thread the fringe
through the chain loops at edge of shawl and tie fringe.

Measurements: Triangle approx
30¾ x 78¾ in / 78 x 200 cm not
including fringe

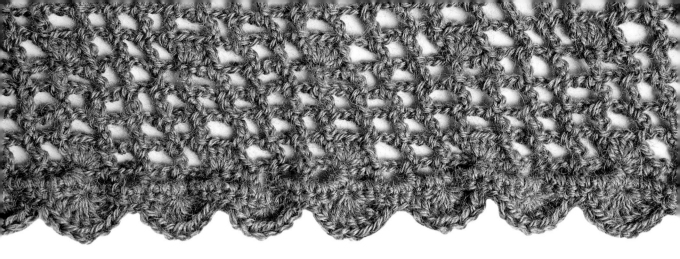

Chain stitch netting shawl with fan patterns

Measurements:
32¼ x 82 in / 82 x 208 cm

Instructions:
Ch 8, 1 tr into 1st ch; turn.
Row 1: Ch 8, 1 sc in loop, ch 3, 1 tr into same loop; turn.
Row 2: Ch 8, 1 sc in loop, 5 dc into sc (= 1 fan), 1 sc in next loop, ch 3, 1 tr in same loop; turn.
Row 3: Ch 8, 1 sc in loop, ch 5, 1 sc into 3rd dc (tip of fan), ch 5, 1 sc in next loop, ch 3, 1 tr in same loop; turn.
Row 4: Ch 8, 1 sc in loop, ch 5, 1 sc in next loop, ch 5, 1 sc in next loop, ch 5, 1 sc in next loop, ch 3, 1 tr in same loop; turn.
Row 5: Ch 8, 1 sc in loop, ch 5, 1 sc in next loop, ch 5, 1 sc in next loop, ch 5, 1 sc in next loop, ch 5, 1 sc in next loop, ch 3, 1 tr in same loop; turn.
Row 6: Ch 8, 1 sc in loop, 5 dc into sc (= fan), 1 sc in loop, ch 5, 1 sc in next loop, ch 5, 1 sc in next loop, ch 5, 1 sc in next loop, 5 dc into sc (= fan), 1 sc in next loop, ch 3, 1 tr in same loop; turn.
Row 7: Ch 8, 1 sc in loop, ch 5, 1 sc into 3rd dc (tip of fan), ch 5, 1 sc in loop, ch 5, 1 sc in next loop, ch 5, 1 sc in next loop, ch 5, 1 sc into 3rd dc (tip of fan), ch 5, 1 sc in next loop, ch 3, 1 tr in same loop; turn.
Row 8: Ch 8, 1 sc in loop, *ch 5, 1 sc in next loop*; rep * to *, ending row with ch 3, 1 tr in same loop; turn.
Row 9: Work as for Row 8: Ch 8, 1 sc in loop, *ch 5, 1 sc in next loop*; rep * to *, ending row with ch 3, 1 tr in same loop; turn.
Row 10: Ch 8, 1 sc in loop *5 dc into sc (= fan), [1 sc in next loop ch 5) 3 times, 1 sc in next loop*; rep * to *, ending row with 5 dc into sc (= fan), 1 sc in next loop, ch 3, 1 tr in same loop; turn.
Row 11: Ch 8, 1 sc into loop; *ch 5, 1 sc into 3rd dc (tip of fan), [ch 5, 1 sc in next loop] 3 times*; rep * to *, ending row with ch 5, 1 sc into 3rd dc (tip of fan), ch 5, 1 sc in next loop, ch 3, 1 tr in same loop; turn.
Row 12: Work as for Row 8.
Row 13: Work as for Row 9.
Row 14: Work as for Row 10.
Row 15: Work as for Row 11.
Repeat these Rows 8-11 (= 4 row repeat) until there are 96-104 loops across row or to desired size. End shawl with Rows 9-10.

Fan Edging:
When shawl is desired size, crochet the edging. Do not cut yarn – continue along diagonal side.
Row 1 (WS): Ch 1, *3 sc in loop*; rep * to * to point of shawl; 7 sc in loop at point, and then work * to * along other side. End row with 3 sc in last loop; turn.
Row 2: Ch 1, *3 sc in sc, skip 2 sc, 7 tr into next sc (= fan), skip 2 sc*; rep * to * to point of shawl. Make a fan with 11 tr into 4th sc (of the 7 sc on loop at point). Work * to * along other side and end with 3 sc. Do not cut yarn.
Continue along the long side of the shawl, crocheting a row with *7 tr into sc (= fan), 1 sc into loop, 1 sc into sc, 1 sc in loop*; rep * to * all along side, ending with 1 sl st into ch at beg of Row 2. Cut yarn.
Weave in all yarn tails neatly on WS and lightly steam press shawl.
Optional Finishing: Knot fringes into each loop on the two diagonal sides. Cut yarn into 11 in / 28 cm lengths and use 2 strands for each fringe. Use a crochet hook to thread the fringe through the chain loops at edge of shawl and tie fringe.

Materials:
Yarn: Sport (CYCA #2)
Shown here: Garnstudio Alpaca (100% alpaca)
182 yds / 167 m, 50 g, seven 50 g balls
lavender-gray 6437
Hook: US D-3 / 3 mm

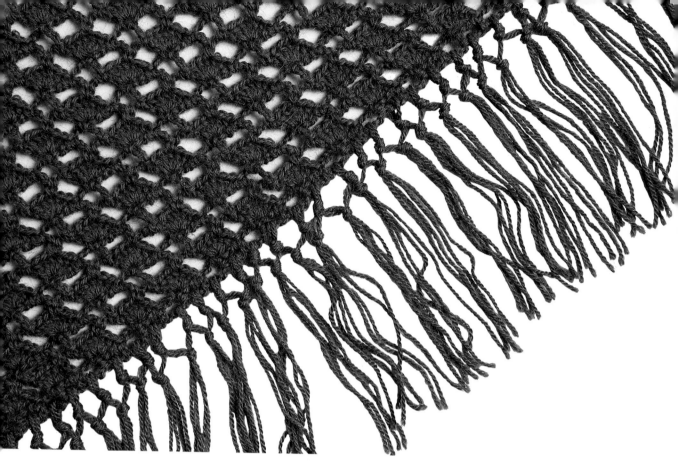

Fan stitch crocheted shawl

Measurements: Triangle approx 30¾ x 78¾ in / 78 x 200 cm not including fringe

Materials:
Yarn: Sport (CYCA #2)
Shown here: Garnstudio Alpaca (100% alpaca)
182 yds / 167 m, 50 g, 400 g dark slate blue 6790
Hook: US D-3 / 3 mm

Instructions:
Ch 8, 1 tr into 1st ch; turn.
Row 1: Ch 8, 1 sc in loop, ch 3, 1 tr into same loop; turn.
Row 2: Ch 8, 1 sc in loop, 5 dc in sc (= fan), 1 sc in next loop, ch 3, 1 tr into same loop; turn.
Row 3: Ch 8, 1 sc in loop, ch 5, 1 sc in 3rd dc (tip of fan), ch 5, 1 sc in next loop, ch 3, 1 tr in same loop; turn.
Row 4: Ch 8, 1 sc in loop, *5 dc in sc (= fan), 1 sc in next loop, ch 5, 1 sc in next loop*; rep * to *, ending row with ch 3, 1 tr into same loop; turn.

Row 5: Ch 8, 1 sc in loop, *ch 5, 1 sc into 3rd dc (tip of fan), ch 5, 1 sc in next loop*; rep * to *, ending row with ch 5, 1 sc in 3rd dc (tip of fan), ch 5, 1 sc in next loop, ch 3, 1 tr into same loop; turn.
Row 6: Work as for Row 4.
Row 7: Work as for Row 5.
Repeat Rows 4-5 (2-row repeat) until there are 114-120 loops across the row or to desired size. finish shawl with Rows 4-5.
Weave in all yarn tails neatly on WS and lightly steam press shawl.

Knot fringes into each loop on the two diagonal sides. Cut yarn into 11 in / 28 cm lengths and use 2 strands for each fringe. Use a crochet hook to thread the fringe through the chain loops at edge of shawl and tie fringe. Next, make a second row of knots by dividing each fringe group into half and knotting 2 strands from one fringe with 2 strands of adjacent fringe.

Crocheted stole/shawl

Materials:
Yarn: Lace weight
Shown here: Tekstilmakeriet Baby Alpaca 20/2 (100% baby alpaca) 10000 m/kg sold in 50 g balls, 547 yds / 500 m, 150 g each gray 0-9411 and beige 0-9207
Substitutions: Misti Alpaca lace (2-ply, 100% baby alpaca) 437 yds, 50 g or Isager Alpaca 1 (100% baby alpaca) 437 yds, 50 g
Hook: US E-4 / 3.5 mm
The stole is worked with 2 strands of yarn held together, one strand of each color.
Gauge: 24 sts in width and 12 rows in length = 4 x 4 in / 10 x 10 cm
Pattern repeat = 10 ch + 7 ch extra for last repeat.

Instructions:

With both colors held together, ch 117.

Row 1: 1 sc into 12th ch from hook, [ch 6, 1 sc in same ch as previous sc] 3 times (= 3 petals), ch 4, skip 4 ch, 1 sc in next ch, *ch 4, skip 4 ch, 1 sc in next ch, [ch 6, 1 sc in same ch as previous sc] 3 times (= 3 petals), ch 4, skip 4 ch, 1 sc in next ch*; rep * to * across; turn.

Row 2: Ch 3, 1 dc in sc, ch 1, skip ch-4 loop, *[1 sc, ch 3, 1 sc = picot, ch 2] in each of the first two ch-6 loops (petals), [1 sc, ch 3, 1 sc = picot] in next ch-6 loop (petal), ch 1**, 1 sc in next ch-4 loop, ch 2, 1 sc in next ch-4 loop, ch 1*; rep * to *, ending last repeat at **. End the row by skipping over the next ch-4 loop, 1 sc in 5th ch in loop; turn.

Row 3: Ch 4 (= 1 dc + 1 ch), 1 sc in 1st picot, *ch 4, 1 sc in next picot, [ch 6, 1 sc in same picot as previous sc] 3 times (3 petals), ch 4, 1 sc in next picot, skip 1 loop**, ch 2, 1 dc in next ch-2 loop, ch 2, skip 1 loop, 1 sc in next 3 picot*; repeat * to *, ending last repeat at **. End row with ch 1, 1 dc into dc; turn.

Row 4: Ch 3, 1 dc in dc, *ch 1, skip ch-4 loop, [1 sc, ch 3, 1 sc = picot, ch 2] in each of the two first ch-6 loops (petals), [1 sc, ch 3, 1 sc = picot] in next ch-6 loop (petal), ch 1, skip ch-4 loop**, 1 sc in next ch-2 loop, ch 2, 1 sc in next ch-2 loop*; rep * to *, ending last repeat at **, 1 sc into 3rd chain of ch-4 loop.

Repeat Rows 3 and 4 alternately until piece is 59 in / 1.5 m long or desired length. End with Row 3.

Next-to-last row: Ch 3, 1 dc in dc, *ch 1, skip ch-4 loop, [1 sc, ch 3, 1 sc = picot, ch 2] in each of the first two ch-6 loops (petals), [1 sc, ch 3, 1 sc = picot] in next ch-6 loop (petal), ch 1, skip ch-4 loop**, 1 sc in next ch-2

loop, (1 sl st, ch 4, 1 sl st) in next dc, 1 sc in next ch-2 loop*; rep * to *, ending last repeat at **, 1 sc into 3rd ch of ch-4 loop.

Last row: Ch 7 (= 1 dc + 4 ch), *1 dc in next ch-3 loop (picot), ch 3, 1 sl st in next ch-3 loop (picot), ch 3, 1 dc in next ch-3 loop (picot) **, ch 3, tr in next ch-4 loop, ch 3*; repeat * to *, ending last repeat at **, ch 4, 1 dc in last dc. Cut yarn.

Pin out shawl on blocking mat or board to about 19¾ x 78¾ in / 50 x 200 cm (see detail photo). Dampen piece and let it dry completely before removing pins (see page 58). The stole will be the finished size once you've crocheted on the edging.

Edging:

1 repeat = 10 sts, 54 repeats are worked along each long side and 15 repeats on each short side.
Round 1: Start at beg of one long side and work 540 sc along edge of long side. At corner, work 10 sc, and

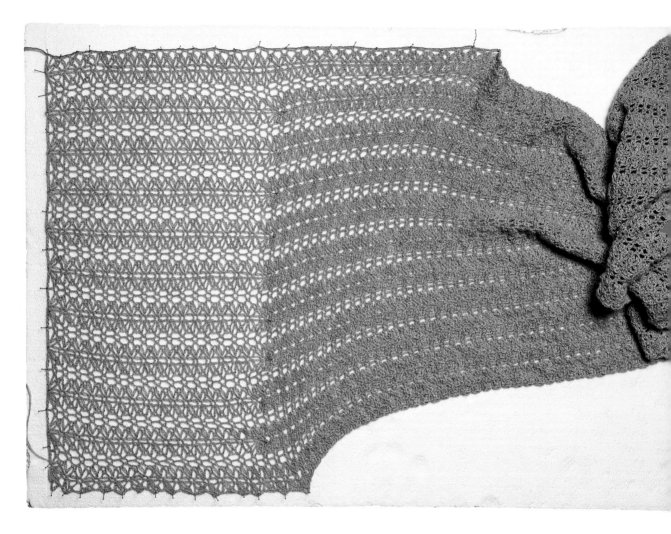

then 150 sc along short side, work corner and then other edges/corners the same way. Adjust stitch counts if necessary to make sure that edge doesn't pucker or ruffle. End rnd with 1 sl st into 1st sc.

Round 2: Ch 1, *(1 sc into next sc) 3 times, ch 1, skip 2 sc, 1 dc in next sc, ch 1, 1 dc in same sc, ch 1, skip 2 sc, 1 sc into each of next 2 sc*; rep * to * on long side (54 repeats on one long edge). In each corner work as follows: 1 sc into each of next 3 sc, ch 1, skip 2 sc, 1 dc in next sc, ch 1, 1 dc in same sc, ch 1, 1 dc in same sc, ch 1, 1 dc in same sc, ch 1, skip 2 sc, 1 sc into each of next 2 sc. Repeat * to * on short side (15 repeats on one short side); work corner sequence in next corner; * to * along long side, corner, and end rnd with 1 sl st into 1st sc.

Round 3: Ch 1, 1 sc into each of next 2 sc, skip 1 sc, ch 1, and 1 dc, 2 dc in next loop, ch 1, 2 dc in same loop, ch 1, skip 1 ch, 1 dc and 1 sc, 1 sc in sc*; repeat * to * down long side. Work each corner as follows: 1 sc in each of next 2 sc, ch 1, skip 1 sc, ch 1, and 1 dc, 2 dc in next ch, ch 1, 2 dc in next ch, ch 1, 2 dc in same loop, ch 1, 2 dc in next sc, ch 1, skip 1 ch, 1 dc, and 1 sc, work 1 sc in next sc. Repeat * to * along next short side, and work corner pattern in next corner, * to *

along long side, corner, and * to * along short side, end with corner and then 1 sl st into 1st sc.

Round 4: Ch 1, 1 sc in next sc, ch 1, skip 1 sc, ch 1 and 2 dc, work 3 dc in next ch, ch 1, 3 dc in same loop, ch 1, skip 1 ch, 2 dc, and 1 sc*; rep * to * along long side. Work each corner as follows: 1 sc in next sc, ch 1, skip 1 sc, work 1 dc in ch-1 loop, ch 1, 1 dc in dc, ch 1, skip 1 dc, work 1 dc in ch-1 loop, ch 1, skip 2 dc, ch 1, 1 dc in ch-1 loop, ch 1, 1 dc in same loop, ch 1, 1 dc in same loop, ch 1, 1 dc in same loop, ch 1, skip 2 dc, 1 dc into ch-1 loop, ch 1, 1 dc in dc, ch 1, skip 1 dc, work 1 dc in ch-1 loop.

Repeat * to * along short side, work corner pattern in next corner, repeat * to * along long side, corner, * to * along short side, and corner. End rnd with 1 sl st into 1st sc.

Round 5: Ch 1, *1 sc in next sc, 1 sc in dc, 1 sc in dc, (ch 3, 1 sl st into ch-1 loop = 1 picot), 1 sc in dc, 1 sc in ch, 1 picot, 1 sc in same ch, 1 sc in dc, 1 picot, 1 sc in dc, 1 sc in dc*; repeat * to * around. Cut yarn.

Weave in all yarn tails neatly on WS and lightly steam press edging under a pressing cloth.

Blanket with flower border

Measurements: approx 43¼ x 74¾ in / 110 x 190 cm

Materials:
Yarn: DK (CYCA #3)
Shown here: Det Mjuke, Kristin (100% Merino wool) 126 yds / 115 m, 50 g, 100 g each Horsetail (Equisetum) 011, cochineal, F6 003, cochineal VI 4 004, madder 012, dyer's rocket V2, 002, indigo B 008, indigo blue 1, 009, walnut 007, pomegranate V6 006, 900 g cucumber 010
Substitutions: Berroco Pure Merino DK (100% Extra Fine Merino) 126 yds / 115 m, 50 g or Louet Gems Sport (100% Merino Wool) slighty heavier 225 yds / 205 m, 100 g
Hook: US J-10 / 6 mm
Gauge: 14 sts = 4 in / 10 cm

Blanket:
With cucumber, ch 126.
Row 1: Beg in 6th ch from hook, *3 dc group in ch, skip 2 ch *, repeat * to * across, ending with 3-dc group in ch.
Row 2: Ch 5, *skip 3-dc group, make 3-dc group between two groups *; repeat * to * across, ending with a 3-dc group into ch-5 loop.
Row 3 and remaining rows: Repeat Row 2 until piece measures 67 in / 170 cm or desired length. Cut yarn.

Tip: Leave all the yarn ends at the side so you can use them to sew on the flowers.

Flowers for the Edging:
Ch 5 and join into a ring with 1 sl st into 1st ch.
Round 1: Ch 5 (= 3 ch + 1 dc), *ch 3, 1 hdc in ring*; rep * to * 7 times and end with 1 sl st into 2nd ch.
Round 2: *1 sc, ch 1, 3 dc, ch 1, 1 sc in ch-3 loop (= 1 petal)*; repeat * to * 8 times and end with 1 sl st into 1st ch.
Round 3: *1 sc into hdc from 1st rnd (crochet around post of hdc), ch 4, 1 sc around hdc from rnd 1 *rep * to * 8 times and end with 1 sl st into 1st sc.
Round 4: Ch 1, *1 sc, ch 2, 5 dc, ch 2, 1 sc in ch-4 loop *; repeat * to * 8 times and end with 1 sl st into 1st sc.
Round 5: *1 sc into sc of rnd 3 (crochet around post of sc), ch 5, 1 sc around sc of rnd 3 *; rep * to * 8 times and end with 1 sl st into 1st sc.
Round 6a: Ch 1, *(1 hdc, 1 st, 5 tr, 1 dc, 1 hdc) into ch-5 loop*; repeat * to * 8 times, ending with 1 sl st into 1st hdc.

Crochet a total of 56 flowers in an assortment of colors. If you want to join the flowers as you work, work Round 6a on the first flower of each row and then work Round 6b for all the other flowers on the row.

Round 6b: Joining two flowers: crochet to the last two petals as explained under 6a and then:
1 hdc, 1 dc, 1 tr, insert hook into the same point on the other flower, and join with 1 sl st, 2 tr, join the flowers again with 1 sl st in the second petal, 2 tr, join again with 1 sl st in the second petal, 2 tr from previous sl st, 1 tr, 1 dc, 1 hdc; repeat * to * on the next petal and end with 1 sl st into 1st hdc.

The next flower is joined through the two petals on the opposite side.

Join the flowers into rows, making 2 rows with 17 flowers in each and 2 rows with 11 flowers each. Sew the two long rows of flowers to the long sides of the blanket, attaching at center of a petal. Finish by sewing the short rows of flowers to short sides of blanket. Instead of crocheting the flowers together, you can sew them together. Lightly steam press flowers under a pressing cloth.

Poncho

Size: Medium
Measurements: total length from back neck to point
= 34 in / 86 cm

Materials:
Yarn: DK, fuzzy (CYCA #3)
Shown here: Garnstudio Kid-Silk (75% super kid mohair/25% silk)
219 yds / 200 m, 25 g, 125 g each light steel blue 07 and beige 12
Hook: US J-9 / 5.5 mm and US H-8 / 5 mm for crab stitch edging
Gauge: 16 sc with doubled yarn and larger hook = 4 in / 10 cm
Poncho is worked with 1 strand of each color held together.

Double Treble Cluster (dbl tr cluster): the number of double
trebles to make for each cluster is indicated by the number before
the abbreviation for the cluster, for example 3-dbl tr cluster.
Paired Double Treble Cluster (paired dbl tr cluster): the number of double trebles to make for each cluster is indicated by the
number before the cluster abbreviation. For example, paired 3-dbl
tr cluster. Work as for a dbl tr cluster to the last step when 3 loops
remain on the hook, skip 5 sc and make a 3-dbl tr cluster and
then finish with yarn around hook and through all 6 loops on the
hook to make 1 stitch from the paired clusters.
Pattern repeat = 6 sts.

Instructions:
Holding 1 strand each light gray-blue and beige
together, ch 62.
Row 1: 1 sc in 2nd ch from hook, 1 sc in each ch
across = 61 sc; turn.
Row 2: Ch 1, 1 sc in each sc across; turn.
Row 3: Ch 1, 1 sc in each sc across; turn.
Row 4: Ch 5 (= 1 dbl tr), skip 2 sc, 3-dbl tr cluster (see
above) into sc, ch 5, paired 3-dbl tr cluster (first half
of paired 3-dbl tr cluster is worked in the same sc as
previous cluster, see photo) *ch 5, paired 3-dbl tr cluster (first half of the paired 3-dbl tr cluster, see photo)*;
repeat * to * across until 3 sc remain, ch 5, 3-dbl tr
cluster in same sc as previous paired cluster, but do not
bring yarn through on last step of stitch, skip 2 sc, 1 dbl
tr in last sc and pull yarn through all 4 dbl tr at the same
time (last dbl tr and 3-dbl tr cluster); turn.

Row 5: Ch 1, 1 sc in tip of 3-dbl cluster, 5 sc in ch-5
loop, *1 sc in tip of paired 3-dbl tr cluster, 5 sc in ch-5
loop*; rep * to * across, ending with 1 sc in tip of 3-dbl
tr cluster; turn.
Row 6: Ch 1, 1 sc in each sc across; turn.
Row 7: Ch 1, 1 sc in each sc across; turn.
Repeat Rows 4-7 throughout (4-row pattern repeat).
Work a total of 15 pattern repeats and then work another piece the same way.

Finishing:
Join the two sections, matching long side against short
side with slip sts or seam by hand. See drawing.

Lower edge:
Round 1: Begin at one point with 3 sc in the same
stitch. Work 1 sc in each sc row and 5 sc into each ch-

5 loop or 1 dbl tr. In the corners, work 3 sc in same st. End round with 1 sl st into 1st sc.

Round 2: Ch 1, 1 sc into each sc. On corners, work 3 sc into same sc. End rnd with 1 sl st into 1st sc.

Round 3: Work as for Rnd 2.

Round 4: Sl st to corner, 3-dbl tr cluster (work ch 5 instead of 1st dbl tr of cluster) into corner, ch 5, 3-dbl tr cluster in same st, ch 5, paired 3-dbl tr cluster (first half of the paired 3-dbl tr cluster is worked in the same sc as for 3-dbl tr cluster), *ch 5, paired 3-dbl tr cluster*; repeat * to * to next corner. In the corner, work 3-dbl tr cluster, ch 5, 3-dbl tr cluster in the same sc; rep * to * to next corner and end round with 1 sl st into 5th ch.

Round 5: Ch 1, 9 sc into ch-5 loop (corner) and then *5 sc into ch-5 loop*; repeat * to * to next corner. In the corner, work 9 sc in ch-5 loop; rep * to * to next corner and end with 1 sl st into ch.

Round 6: Ch 1, 1 sc in each sc around, except at corners where you should work 3 sc into 1 sc at tip. End with 1 sl st into ch.

Rounds 7-11: Work as for Rnd 6.

Round 12: Change to smaller hook (this makes the edging a bit tighter). Ch 1, 1 crab st in each sc around, ending with 1 sl st into 1st crab st. Cut yarn.

Edging around Neckline

Round 1: Work 1 sc into each sc across and 5 sc into ch-5 loop or 1 dbl tr. End with 1 sl st into 1st sc.

Round 2: Ch 1, *1 sc into next sc 5 times, dec 1 sc by working the next 2 sc together*; repeat * to * to next corner. Work the last sc before the corner and the first sc after corner together to 1 sc; rep * to * to next corner, and end round with 1 sl st into ch.

Round 3: Ch 1, 1 sc in each sc around but decrease at each corner as for Rnd 2.

Round 4: Change to smaller hook (for a tighter edging), ch 1, 1 crab st in each sc around and end with 1 sl st into 1st crab st. Cut yarn. Weave in all yarn tails neatly on WS and light steam press poncho.

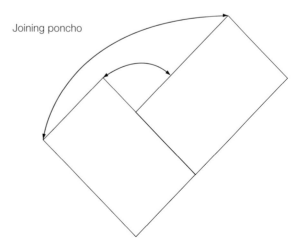

Joining poncho

Felted cushions

Adult-size felted cushion

Instructions:

With color 1, ch 53.

Row 1: 1 hdc in 3rd ch from hook, 1 hdc in each ch across = 50 hdc; turn.

Row 2: Ch 2, 1 hdc in each hdc across = 50 hdc / turn.

Row 3: Work as for Row 2. If you want a handle for your cushion, see below for alternate Rows 3 and 4.

Row 4: Work as for Row 2.

Row 5: Change to color 3 and work as for Row 2.

Rows 6-9: Work as for Row 2.

Row 10: Change to color 1 and work as for Row 2.

Row 11: Work as for Row 2.

Row 12: Change to color 2 and work as for Row 2.

Rows 13-17: Work as for Row 2.

Row 18: Change to color 3 and work as for Row 2.

Row 19: Work as for Row 2.

Row 20: Change to color 2 and work as for Row 2.

Rows 21-25: Work as for Row 2.

Row 26: Change to color 1 and work as for Row 2.

Row 27: Work as for Row 2.

Row 28: Change to color 3 and work as for Row 2.

Rows 29-32: Work as for Row 2.

Row 33: Change to color 1 and work as for Row 2.

Rows 34-36: Work as for Row 2.

Handle:

Row 3: Work Row 3 as follows: Ch 2, 1 hdc in each of next 18 hdc, ch 14, skip 14 hdc, 1 hdc in each of next 18 hdc (to end of row); turn.

Row 4: Work as follows: Ch 2, 1 hdc in each of next 18 hdc, 1 hdc in each of next 14 ch, 1 hdc in each of next 18 hdc (to end of row); turn.

Crocheted Edging:

Round 1: Side 1: Begin on the long side with purple and work 1 sc in each hdc; at the corner, work 3 sc. Side 2 (short side): 1 sc at beg of each row along the short side, making sure that the edge doesn't pucker or ruffle. Work 3 sc into corner st. Repeat sides 1 and 2 on the other two sides and end round with 1 sl st into 1st ch.

Round 2: Ch 1, 1 sc in each sc around; at each corner, work 2 sc in the center of the 3 sc. End round with 1 sl st into ch. Cut yarn.

Finishing:

Weave in all yarn tails neatly on WS.

Measurements before felting:
approx 24½ x 20½ in / 62 x 52 cm

Measurements after felting:
approx 17¾ x 15 in / 45 x 38 cm

Materials:

Yarn: Bulky, single ply (CYCA #5)
Shown here: Garnstudio Eskimo (100% wool) 55 yds / 50 m, 50 g, 100 g orange rust 07 = color 1; 150 g orchid 04 = color 2; 100 g orange/purple/red 19p = color 3

Hook: US N/P 15 / 10 mm

Felting:

Felt the cushion in the washing machine. Use a wool wash, such as Eucalan or Soak, and complete washing cycle. Set temperature for pre-wash at 104°F/40°C. Put 3 tennis balls into the washer with the cushion to facilitate the felting process.

Child-size felted cushion

Measurements before felting:
approx 16½ x 20 in / 42 x 51 cm
Measurements after felting:
approx 12¼ x 14½ in / 31 x 37 cm

Materials:
Yarn: Bulky, single ply (CYCA #5)
Shown here: Garnstudio Eskimo (100% wool) 55 yds /
50 m, 50 g, 100 g amethyst mix 36 = color 1;
150 g dark blue/purple 39 = color 2; 100 g rosybrown/
heather print 43p = color 3
Hook: US N/P 15 / 10 mm

Instructions:
With color 1, ch 43 and continue with that color until the
yarn runs out or you want to change colors.
Row 1: 1 hdc in 3rd ch from hook and then 1 hdc in
each ch across = 41 hdc; turn.
Row 2: Ch 2, 1 hdc in each hdc across = 41 hdc; turn.
Rows 3-28: Work as for Row 2. If you want a handle for
your cushion, see below for alternate Rows 3 and 4.

Handle:
Row 3: Work Row 3 as follows: Ch 2, 1 hdc in each of
next 15 hdc, ch 11, skip 11 hdc, 1 hdc in each of next
15 hdc (to end of row); turn.
Row 4: Work as follows: Ch 2, 1 hdc in each of next 15
hdc, 1 hdc in each of next 11 ch, 1 hdc in each of next
15 hdc (to end of row); turn.

Crocheted Edging:
Round 1: Side 1: Begin on the long side with grape and
work 1 sc in each hdc; at the corner, work 3 sc.
Side 2 (short side): 1 sc at beg of each row along the
short side, making sure that the edge doesn't pucker
or ruffle. Work 3 sc into corner st. Repeat sides 1 and
2 on the other two sides and end round with 1 sl st into
1st ch.
Round 2: Ch 1, 1 sc in each sc around; at each corner,
work 2 sc in the center of the 3 sc. End round with 1 sl
st into ch. Cut yarn.

Finishing:
Weave in all yarn tails neatly on WS.

Felting:
See explanation for felting in pattern for adult cushion.

Materials:
Yarn: DK (CYCA #3)
Shown here: daVibe, Hemp yarn, 400 g
natural 1 mm
Substitution: Hempnatural # 130 hemp
12 (100% hemp natural yarn) 425 yds /
393 m, 500g
Hook: US E-4 and 7 / 3.5 and 4.5 mm
The hemp yarn can stretch so be careful
not to crochet too loosely.

Crocheted shopping bag

Instructions:

With smaller hook, ch 5 and join into a ring with sl st.

Round 1: Work 6 sc around ring. Join with 1 sl st in 1st sc.

Round 2: Ch 1, 2 sc in each sc around = 12 sc; join with 1 sl st in 1st ch.

Round 3: Ch 1, *2 sc into next sc, 1 sc in next sc*; rep * to * around = 18 sc; join with 1 sl st in 1st ch.

Round 4: Ch 1, *2 sc into next sc, 1 sc each in next 2 sc*; rep * to * around = 24 sc; join with 1 sl st in 1st ch.

Round 5: Ch 1, *2 sc into next sc, 1 sc each in next 3 sc*; rep * to * around = 30 sc; join with 1 sl st in 1st ch.

Round 6: Ch 1, *2 sc into next sc, 1 sc each in next 4 sc*; rep * to * around = 36 sc; join with 1 sl st in 1st ch.

Round 7: Ch 1, *2 sc into next sc, 1 sc each in next 5 sc*; rep * to * around = 42 sc; join with 1 sl st in 1st ch.

Rep Rnd 7 until there are 12 sc between increases, working 1 more sc between increases on each round (6 sts are increased on each round).

Work 1 rnd with 1 sc in each sc around (no increases). Work 1 rnd crab st into front loop only in each sc around (crab st = sc worked from left to right). The base of the bag is now complete.

Change to larger hook, work the sides of the bag:

Round 1: Ch 2, 1 hdc into back loop of each sc around; join with 1 sl st into 1st sc (the crab st edging forms a welt around the base).

Round 2: Ch 2, 1 hdc in each hdc (work through both loops) and end rnd with 1 sl st into 2nd ch.

Repeat Rnd 2 until side is 13 in / 33 cm long. Cut yarn. To position strap, place a marker at beginning and center of rnd. Count out 18 sts before beg of rnd. Begin strap here.

Row 1: Work 36 hdc; turn.

Row 2: Ch 1, decrease 1 by working first two hdc tog, and then work 1 hdc in each st across to last 2 hdc; dec by working last 2 hdc tog = 34 hdc.

Row 3: Work as for Row 2 = 32 hdc.

Row 4: Work as for Row 2 = 30 hdc.

Repeat Row 4 until 8 hdc rem and then continue back and forth over these 8 hdc, beginning each row with ch 2. Work until strap is 15 in / 38 cm long. Cut yarn. Crochet the other side of the strap the same way, beginning 18 sts before the center marker. When strap is 15 in / 38 cm long, join the short ends of the straps with sl st across. Cut yarn.

On each side of strap, work a round of sc around top of bag and strap edge. Weave in all yarn tails neatly on WS.

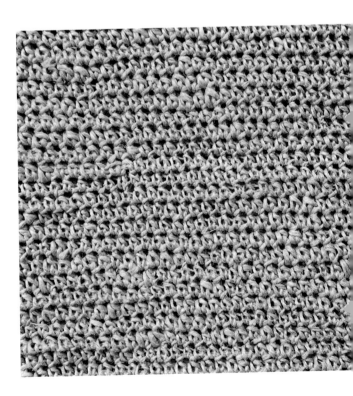

Crocheted net bag

Materials:
Yarn:
Shown here: Tekstilmakeriet, Bocken's tow yarn
(100% linen) Nel 8 = 1250 m / 250 g for unbleached
and 1400 g / 150 g for bleached and dyed
8 spools (250 g each) dark natural 2048
Substitution: Borgs Tow yarn
Hook: US 6 / 1.75 mm

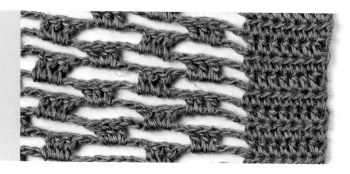

Instructions:
With 2 strands of yarn held together, ch 226.
Row 1: Beg in 3rd ch from hook (= 1 hdc), 1 hdc in
each of next 9 ch, *ch 6, skip 6 ch, 1 dc in each of next
3 ch*; rep * to * 22 times, ch 6, skip 6 ch, 1 hdc in each
of next 10 ch; turn.
Row 2: Ch 2 (= 1 hdc), 1 hdc in each of next 9 hdc, ch
3, *3 dc around ch loop, ch 6, skip 3 dc*; rep * to * 22
times, 3 dc around loop, ch 3, 1 hdc in each of next 10
hdc; turn.
Row 3: Ch 2 (= 1 hdc), 1 hdc in each of next 9 hdc,
ch 6, skip 3 dc, 3 dc around next ch loop; rep * to *
22 times, ch 6, skip 3 dc, 1 hdc in each of next 10 hdc;
turn.
Row 4: Work as for Row 2.
Row 5: Work as for Row 3.

Repeat Rows 2-3 until piece is 11 in / 28 cm long (mea-
sure along hdc edge); do not cut yarn.

Pin out piece to aprox 11 x 29¼ in / 28 x 74 cm on a
blocking mat or board (see detail photo). Dampen and
let dry completely before removing pins. The bag must
be blocked before seaming the sides (see detail photo).
When the bag is dry, crochet the straps.
Strap: Continue with hdc over hdc: ch 2 (= 1 hdc) 1 hdc
in each of next 9 hdc; turn; repeat this row until strap is
16½ in / 42 cm long. Join strap to opposite side of bag
with sl st. Make the other strap the same way.
Joining sides: Begin where the strap is joined. Work (8
sc around ch-6 loop, 3 sc into dc) 3 times, 8 sc around
next loop, (ch 9, skip 3 dc, 1 sc in next ch loop) 9 times.
You are now at the base of the bag and the sides have
been seamed. Ch 4, 1 sc in next-to-last ch-9 loop

which was crocheted earlier on the row, ch 4, (1 sc in
next loop, ch 4, 1 sc into next ch-9 loop that was made
earlier on row, ch 4) 6 times, (8 sc around next ch loop,
3 sc in dc) 3 times and end with 8 sc over last ch loop.
Cut yarn. Weave in yarn tails neatly on WS.

Potholders
and dishrags

Measurements Potholder:
approx 8 x 8 in / 20 x 20 cm
Measurements Dishrag:
approx 11½ x 11½ in / 29 x 29 cm

Materials for Potholders:
Yarn: Worsted, plied (CYCA #4)
Shown here: Garnstudio Bomull-Lin Cotton/Linen
(53% cotton/47% linen) 93 yds / 85 m, 50 g
100 g each brown 05 and beige 03, and Muskat
(100% cotton), 50 g red 12 for edging.
Hook: US E-4 / 3.5 mm

Instructions for Pothholders:

With either color cotton/linen yarn, ch 47.

Row 1: Work 1 dc in 3rd ch from hook and then 1 dc in each ch across = 45 dc; turn.

Row 2: Ch 3 (= 1 dc) *1 dc around post of the 2nd dc from previous row, 1 dc around post of next dc from previous row, 1 dc in dc, 1 dc in dc*; rep * to * across and end with 1 dc; turn.

Rows 3-25 (or until potholder is squared): Work as for Row 2.

Edging:

Change to Muskat red cotton yarn.

Round 1:

Side 1: *1 sc in 2nd dc, ch 2, skip 2 dc*; rep * to * until 1 st from corner, ch 7.

Side 2: Skip 1 st, *1 sc, ch 2; rep * to * with sts evenly spaced along the side so that the edging doesn't pull in or pucker. Ch 7 at corner.

Repeat Sides 1 and 2 on other side of potholder and end rnd with 1 sl st into 1st sc.

Round 2:

Side 1: *1 sc into 1st ch loop, ch 3, 1 sc into 1st ch (= picot)*; rep * to * along side, ending with 10 sc into 7-ch loop at corner.

Work other 3 sides as for Side 1 and end rnd with 1 sl st into 1st sc.

Make another potholder the same way using the alternate main color. Weave in yarn tails neatly on WS.

Materials for Dishrags:

Yarn:

Shown here: Tekstilmakeriet, Bocken's 16/2 linen yarn (100% linen) unbleached is 4920 m/kg and bleached and dyed 5520 m/kg, 1 spool each natural 0000-unbleached or dark natural 462 and red 1007

Substitution: Bochens yarn

Hook: US A-B / 2-2.5 mm

Tip: Crochet the dishrag a bit loosely.

Instructions for Dishrags:

With your choice of main color, ch 107. Beg in 3rd ch from hook.

Row 1: Dc 105 across; turn.

Row 2: Ch 3 (= 1 dc), *1 dc around post of 2nd dc from previous row, 1 dc around post of next dc from previous row, 1 dc in dc, 1 dc in dc*; rep * to * across, ending with 1 dc; turn.

Repeat Row 2 until dishrag is squared.

With red, work edging around dishrag as for potholder. Weave in yarn tails neatly on WS.

Cotton placemats

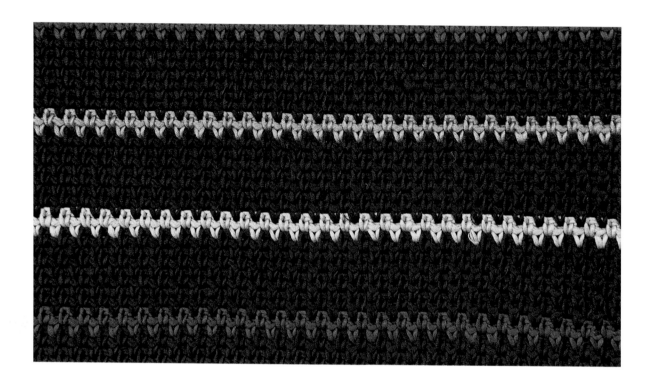

Placemat with simple stripes

Instructions:

With black, ch 88.

Row 1: Sc in 2nd ch from hook, *ch 1, skip 1 ch, 1 sc in next ch*; rep * to * across; turn.

Row 2: Ch 1, 1 sc in next sc, *1 sc in ch, ch 1, skip 1 sc*; rep * to * and end row with 1 sc in ch, 1 sc in sc; turn.

Row 3: Ch 1, 1 sc in next sc, *ch 1, skip 1 sc, 1 sc in ch*; rep from * to * and end row with ch 1, 1 sc in sc; turn.

Row 4: Work as for Row 2.

Row 5: Work as for Row 3.

Repeat Rows 2 and 3 throughout.

At the same time, work stripe sequence as follows: *8 rows black, 2 rows heather, 8 rows black, 2 rows light olive, 8 rows black, 2 rows purple*; rep * to * once and then end with 8 rows black.

Edging:

Rnd 1: Begin at one corner with black and work ch 1 and 2 sc in corner.

Side 1 (top of placemat): 1 sc in each sc and ch along side, work 3 sc in next corner.

Side 2 (side of placemat): 1 sc in about every row and 3 sc in corner.

Side 3 (bottom edge of placemat): 1 sc in each ch (beginning chain) and 3 sc in corner.

Side 4: Work as for Side 2 and end round with 1 sl st into 1st ch.

Rnd 2: Ch 1, 1 crab st in each sc around; end with 1 slip st into 1st crab st. Cut yarn.

Finishing:

Weave in all tails neatly on WS. Lightly steam press placemat.

Measurements: approx
12¾ x 16¼ in / 32.5 x 41 cm

Materials:
Yarn: Worsted, plied
(CYCA #4)
Shown here: Garnstudio
Muskat (100% Egyptian
mercerized cotton)
109 yds / 100m, 50 g)
150 g black 17, 50 g each
heather 39, purple 04,
and light olive 45.
Hook: US size E-4 /
3.5 mm

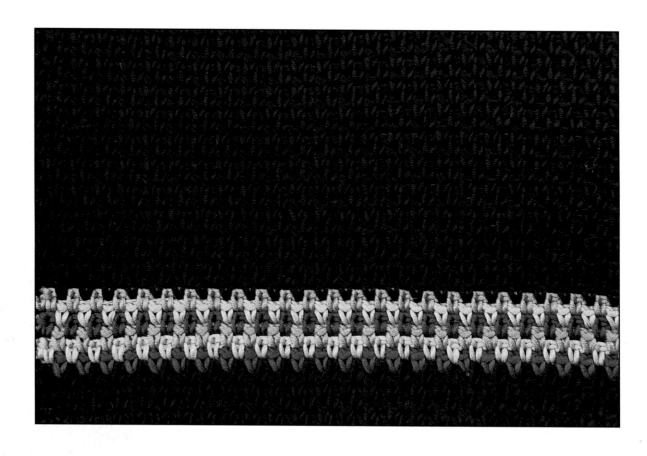

Placemats with striped borders

Instructions:

With black, ch 88.

Row 1: 1 sc in 2nd ch from hook, *ch 1, skip 1 ch, 1 sc in ch*; rep * to * across; turn.

Row 2: Ch 1, 1 sc in next sc, *1 sc in ch, ch 1, skip 1 sc*; rep * to * across, ending row with 1 sc in ch, 1 sc in sc; turn.

Row 3: Ch 1, 1 sc in next sc, *ch 1, skip 1 sc, 1 sc in ch*; rep * to * across, ending row with ch 1, 1 sc in sc; turn.

Row 4: Work as for Row 2.

Row 5: Work as for Row 3.

Repeat Rows 2 and 3 throughout.

At the same time, work stripe sequence as follows:

6 rows black, 1 row heather, 1 row light olive, 1 row purple, 1 row heather, 1 row light olive, 1 row purple, 42 rows black (or 7¼ in / 18.5 cm black), 1 row purple, 1 row light olive, 1 row heather, 1 row purple, 1 row light olive, 1 row heather, and end with 6 rows black.

Edging:

Rnd 1: Begin at one corner with black and work ch 1 and 2 sc in corner.

Side 1 (top of placemat): 1 sc in each sc and ch along side, work 3 sc in next corner.

Side 2 (side of placemat): 1 sc in about every row and 3 sc in corner.

Side 3 (bottom edge of placemat): 1 sc in each ch (beginning chain) and 3 sc in corner.

Side 4: Work as for Side 2 and end round with 1 sl st into 1st ch.

Rnd 2: Change to heather, ch 1, 1 sc in each sc around, but, in each corner, work 3 sc in corner st; end rnd with 1 sl st into 1st ch.

Rnd 3: 1 crab st in each sc around; end with 1 sl st into 1st crab st. Cut yarn.

Finishing:

Weave in all tails neatly on WS. Lightly steam press placemat.

Measurements: approx
12¾ x 16 in / 32.5 x 41 cm

Materials:
Yarn: Worsted,
plied (CYCA #4)
Shown here: Garnstudio
Muskat (100% Egyptian
mercerized cotton) 109 yds / 100 m,
50 g, 100 g black 17, 50 g each
heather 39, purple 04, light olive 45
Hook: US E-4 / 3.5 mm

Measurements:
approx 12¾ x 16½ in / 32 x 42
cm; 1 block measures 2 x 2 in /
5 x 5 cm

Linen granny square placemats

Instructions:

With gray-blue (all blocks), ch 6 and join into a ring with 1 sl st.

Round 1: Continue with gray-blue (all blocks), ch 6 (= 1 dc + 3 ch) [3 dc around ring, ch 3] 3 times, 2 dc around ring, end rnd with 1 sl st into 3rd ch of the ch-6 at beg of rnd. Cut yarn.

Round 2: Change to blue (block 1) or pink (block 2), ch 6 (= 1 dc + ch 3), 3 dc around same ch-loop, *ch 1, [3 dc, ch 3, 3 dc] into next ch-loop*; rep * to * 2 times, ch 1, 2 dc in same ch-loop as beg ch-6. End rnd with 1 sl st in 3rd ch of the ch-6 at beg of rnd. Cut yarn.

Round 3: Change to pink (block 1) or blue (block 2), ch 6 (= 1 dc + ch 3), 3 dc around same ch-loop, *ch 1, 3 dc around next loop, ch 1**, [3 dc, ch 3, 3 dc] into next ch-loop*; rep * 2 times and from * to * * 1 time, 2 dc in same ch-loop as beg ch-6. End rnd with 1 sl st in 3rd ch of the ch-6 at beg of rnd. Cut yarn.

Round 4: Change to natural (block 1) or dark natural (block 2), ch 6 (= 1 dc + ch 3), 3 dc into same ch-loop, *ch 1, [3 dc around next loop, ch 1] 2 times**, [3 dc, ch 3, 3 dc] into next ch-loop*; rep from * 2 times and * to * * 1 time, 2 dc in same ch-loop as beg ch-6. End rnd with 1 sl st in 3rd ch of the ch-6 at beg of rnd. Cut yarn.

Finishing:

With natural, crochet the blocks together on the WS as follows:

Place blocks 1 and 2 with RS facing RS (see drawing for arrangement of blocks). Begin joining at one corner with 1 sc through loops of both blocks, *ch 1, skip 1 ch, 1 sl st into dc through both blocks, ch 1, skip 1 dc, 1 sl st in dc through both blocks*; rep * to * to corner. At corner, work 1 sc through loops on both blocks; do not cut yarn. Place block 3, edge to edge on next side of block 1, RS facing RS. Continue to work 1 sc through loops on both blocks, *ch 1, skip 1 ch, 1 sl st through both blocks, ch 1, skip 1 dc, 1 sl st in dc through both blocks*; rep * to * to corner. At corner work 1 sc through loops of both blocks; cut yarn and weave in ends neatly on WS. Continue, joining blocks 4, 5, and 6 to blocks 2 and 3 (see drawing). See drawing for diagonal sequence of joining blocks. Cut yarn.

Materials:

Yarn:

Shown here: Tekstilmakeriet, Bocken's 16/2 linen yarn (100% linen) unbleached is 4920 m/kg and bleached and dyed 5520 m/kg

Substitution: Bochens yarn

Hook: US A / 2 mm

The placemat consists of 48 blocks. Make 24 blocks each of block color combinations 1 and 2.

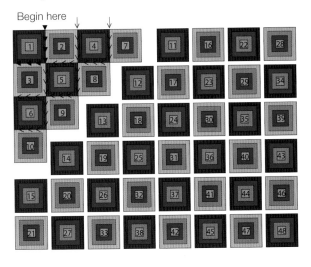

Joining the blocks of the placemat

Begin here

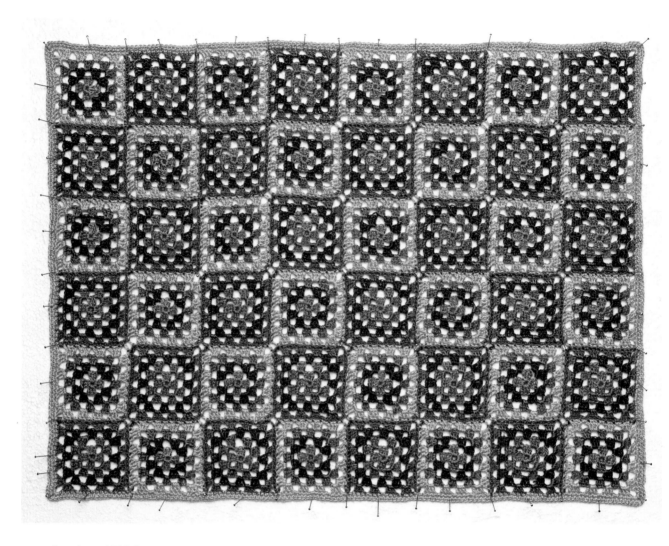

Crocheted Edging:

Round 1: With natural, begin on one long side and work 1 sc into each dc and loop across. At the corner work 5 sc around loop. End rnd with 1 sl st into 1st sc.

Round 2: Ch 1, and then work 1 sc in each sc around; at corners, work 2 sc into the center of the 5 sc at corner. End rnd with 1 sl st into 1st sc. Cut yarn. Weave in all tails neatly on WS.

Pin placemat on a blocking mat or board to approx 12¾ x 16½ in / 32 x 42 cm (see detail photo). Dampen mat and do not remove pins until piece is completely dry.

Containers

Large basket with handles

Measurements: approx 6¾ in / 17 cm diameter, height approx 5½ in / 14 cm

Instructions:

Ch 4 and join into a ring with sl st.

Round 1: Ch 2, 7 hdc around ring and end with 1 sl st into 2nd ch.

Round 2: Ch 2, 1 hdc into same ch, and then 2 hdc in each hdc around; end with 1 sl st into 2nd ch = 16 hdc around.

Round 3: Ch 2, 1 hdc in same ch, 1 hdc in next hdc, *2 hdc in next hdc, 1 hdc in next hdc*; rep * to * around and end with 1 sl st in 2nd ch = 24 hdc.

Round 4: Ch 2, 1 hdc in same ch, 1 hdc each in next 2 hdc, *2 hdc in next hdc, 1 hdc each in next 2 hdc*; rep * to * around and end with 1 sl st in 2nd ch = 32 hdc.

Round 5: As for Rnd 4 but with 3 hdc between increases = 40 hdc.

Round 6: As for Rnd 4 but with 4 hdc between increases = 48 hdc.

Round 7: As for Rnd 4 but with 5 hdc between increases = 56 hdc.

Round 8: As for Rnd 4 but with 6 hdc between increases = 64 hdc.

Round 9: As for Rnd 4 but with 7 hdc between increases = 72 hdc.

Round 10: As for Rnd 4 but with 8 hdc between increases = 80 hdc.

Round 11: As for Rnd 4 but with 9 hdc between increases = 88 hdc.

Round 12: As for Rnd 4 but with 10 hdc between increases = 96 hdc.

Round 13: Ch 1, 1 sc in each hdc, working into back loops only; end with 1 sl st into 1st ch.

Round 14: Ch 1, *in next sc, work 1 dc into back loop only, 1 sc into next sc*; rep * to * around, and end with 1 sl st into 1st ch.

Round 15: Ch 1, *1 sc into dc, 1 dc into back loop of next sc*; rep * to * around and end with 1 sl st in 1st ch.

Round 16: Work as for Rnd 14.

Round 17: Work as for Rnd 15.

Repeat Rnds 14 and 15 until basket is 4 in / 10 cm high. Make the handles on the next round.

Materials:
Yarn: Worsted, plied (CYCA #4)
Shown here: Garnstudio Bomull-Lin Cotton/Linen (53% cotton/47% linen) 93 yds / 85 m, 50 g, 100 g beige 03
Hook: US E-4 / 3.5 mm

Handles:

Work 17 sts in pattern and then ch 15, skip 15 sts, work 33 sts in pattern, ch 15, skip 15 sts, work 16 sts in pattern.

Next round: Work in pattern over all sts and ch-loops. Repeat Rnds 14 and 15 for another 1½ in / 4 cm after handles.

Last Round: Ch 1, 1 crab st in each sc and dc around, ending with 1 sl st into 1st crab st. Cut yarn and weave in all tails neatly on WS.

White basket

Measurements: approx 4 in / 10 cm diameter, height approx 3¼ in / 8.5 cm

Materials:

Yarn: Worsted, plied (CYCA #4)

Shown here: Garnstudio Bomull-Lin Cotton/Linen (53% cotton/47% linen) 93 yds / 85 m, 50 g, 50 g white 01

Hook: US E-4 / 3.5 mm

Instructions:

Ch 4 and join into a ring with sl st.

Round 1: Ch 2, 7 hdc in ring; end rnd with 1 sl st into 2nd ch.

Round 2: Ch 2, 1 hdc in same ch, and then 2 hdc in each hdc around, ending with 1 sl st into 2nd ch = 16 hdc.

Round 3: Ch 2, 1 hdc in same ch, 1 hdc in next hdc, *2 hdc in next hdc, 1 hdc in next hdc*; rep * to * around, and end with 1 sl st in 2nd ch = 24 hdc.

Round 4: Ch 2, 1 hdc in same ch, 1 hdc each in next 2 hdc, *2 hdc in next hdc, 1 hdc each in next 2 hdc*; rep * to * around and end with 1 sl st in 2nd ch = 32 hdc.

Round 5: As for Rnd 4 but with 3 hdc between increases = 40 hdc.

Round 6: As for Rnd 4 but with 4 hdc between increases = 48 hdc.

Round 7: As for Rnd 4 but with 5 hdc between increases = 56 hdc.

Round 8: Ch 1, 1 sc in each hdc, working into back loops only; end with 1 sl st into 1st ch.

Round 9: Ch 1, *work 1 dc into back loop of next sc, 1 sc into next sc*; rep * to * around, and end with 1 sl st into 1st ch.

Round 10: Ch 1, *sc in dc. 1 dc into back loop of next sc*; rep * to * around and end with 1 sl st in 1st ch.

Round 11: Work as for Rnd 9.

Round 12: Work as for Rnd 10

Repeat Rnds 9 and 10 until basket is 3¼ in / 8 cm high. Now work 1 rnd with (ch 1, 1 sc) in each sc and dc around, ending with 1 sl st into 1st ch. Work another 4 rounds with 1 sc into each sc around.

Last Rnd: Ch 1, 1 crab st in each sc around; end with 1 sl st into 1st crab st. Cut yarn. Turn basket inside out and fold brim down to sc edge. Weave in all ends neatly on WS.

Natural white pillows
in various stitch patterns

Pillows 1 and 2

Materials for 1 pillow:
Yarn: Worsted (CYCA #4)
Shown here: Du Store Alpakka, Misti (100% alpaca)
55 yds / 50 m, 550 g natural white 401
Substitutions: Mirasol Sulka (60% Merino/20%
alpaca/20% silk) 55 yds / 50 g; Blue Sky Alpaca
Worsted (50% alpaca/50% wool) 100 yds / 100 g
Pillow forms: 19¾ x 19¾ / 50 x 50 cm
Hook: US J-10 / 6 mm
Gauge: 13 sc = 4 in / 10 cm

Measurements: approx 18½ x 18½ in / 47 x 47 cm
(inner pillow 19¾ x 19¾ / 50 x 50 cm)

Pillows 1 and 2 are crocheted the same way. By
turning one pillow front so that the reverse side
becomes the right side, the pillows have two very
different looks.

Instructions:
Ch 124 and join into a ring with sl st.
Round 1: Ch 1, 1 sc in each ch around, and end with 1
sl st into 1st ch.
Round 2: Ch 1, *1 dc (into back loop only) in next sc, 1
sc in next sc*; rep * to * around and end with 1 sl st into
1st ch.
Round 3: Ch 1, *1 sc in next dc, 1 dc (into back loop
only) of next sc*; rep * to * around and end with 1 sl st
into 1st ch.
Repeat Rnds 2 and 3 until piece is 18½ in / 47 cm long.

Finishing:
Pillow 1: Weave in all ends neatly on WS. Fold pillow
evenly and crochet together with 1 sl st through sts
from both sides or sew by hand (leave bottom edge
open). Insert pillow form and join lower edge with sl st
or by hand.
Pillow 2: Weave in all ends neatly on WS. This pillow
is turned inside out before seaming, so that the WS
becomes the RS. Fold pillow cover and crochet or sew
by hand to seam as for pillow 1.

Pillow 3

Instructions:
Front:
Ch 59.

Row 1: Work 1 dc in 4th ch from hook and then 1 dc into each ch across = 56 dc; turn.

Row 2: *Ch 3 (= 1 dc), (1 dc worked by inserting hook from front to back around post of dc in previous row) 4 times, (1 dc by inserting hook from back to front around post of dc in previous row) 4 times*; rep * to * across; turn.

Row 3: *Ch 3 (= 1 dc), (1 dc worked by inserting hook from front to back around post of dc in previous row) 4 times, (1 dc by inserting hook from back to front around post of dc in previous row) 4 times*; rep * to * across; turn.

Row 4: *Ch 3 (= 1 dc), (1 dc worked by inserting hook from back to front around post of dc in previous row) 4 times, (1 dc by inserting hook from front to back around post of dc in previous row) 4 times*; rep * to * across; turn.

Row 5: *Ch 3 (= 1 dc), (1 dc worked by inserting hook from back to front around post of dc in previous row) 4 times, (1 dc by inserting hook from front to back around post of dc in previous row) 4 times*; rep * to * across; turn.

Repeat Rows 2-5 until piece measures 17 in / 43 cm, ending on either Row 3 or Row 5.

Back:
Ch 50.

Row 1: Beg in 2nd ch from hook, sc 49 across ch; turn.

Row 2: Ch 1 (= 1 sc), 1 sc in back loop in each sc across; turn.

Row 3: Work as for Row 2.

Repeat Rows 2 and 3 until piece is about 13½ in / 34 cm long. The back will be stretched to 17 in / 43 cm during finishing.

Finishing:
Weave in all ends neatly on WS. Place front and back with WS facing WS and pin so that back stretches to same measurements as front. Join pieces together with sc by holding work with front facing you. Begin on side of lower edge. Single crochet up the side (see Note below about corners), across the top, and down on the other side. Note: Work 2 sc in each corner so that the edge doesn't pull in. After you've worked sc down the second side, work back up that side, across the top, and down the other side in crab st. Cut yarn and weave in ends. Insert pillow form and join lower edge with sl st and then work back over each side of the edging with crab st. Cut yarn and weave in ends.

Materials for 1 pillow:
Yarn: Worsted (CYCA #4)
Shown here: Du Store Alpakka, Misti (100% alpaca) 55 yds / 50 m, 700 g natural white 401
Substitutions: Mirasol Sulka (60% Merino/20% alpaca/20% silk) 55 yds / 50 g; Blue Sky Alpaca Worsted (50% alpaca/50% wool) 100 yds / 100 g
Pillow forms: 17¾ x 17¾ / 45 x 45 cm
Hook: US J-10 / 6 mm
Gauge: 13 sc = 4 in / 10 cm

Measurements: approx 17 x 17 / 43 x 43 cm (inner pillow 17¾ x 17¾ / 45 x 45 cm)

Yarn Information

Garnstudio Yarns
Yellow Dog Knitting
420 S. Barstow St.
Eau Claire, WI 54701
715-839-7272
www.yellowdogknitting.com
www.garnstudio.com

Garnstudio DROPS available at:
Nordic Mart
San Luis Obispo, CA, US
805-542-9303
www.nordicmart.com

WEBS – America's Yarn Store
75 Service Center Road
Northampton, MA 01060
800-367-9327
www.yarn.com
customerservice@yarn.com

Vävstuga Swedish Weaving & Folk Arts
16 Water Street
Shelburne Falls, MA 01370
413-625-8241
www.vavstuga.com
Bockens 16/2 Line Linen yarn measures as follows
with a +/- of 5%:
  - *Unbleached/Oblekt 250g/8.8ozs spool*
    1230 meters/1345 yards
  - *1/2 Bleached/1/2 Blekt 250g/8.8ozs spool*
    1380 meters/1509 yards
  - *Dyed/Fargat 125g/4.4ozs spool*
    690 meters/755 yards
Borgs Tow yarn measures as follows with a +/- of 5%:
  - *6/1 Unbleached/Oblekt 250g/8.8ozs spool*
    915 meters/997 yards
  - *6/1 1/2 Bleached/Dyed 250g/8.8ozs spool*
    1088 meters/1186 yards
  - *8/1 Unbleached/Oblekt 250g/8.8ozs spool*
    1212 meters/1321 yards
  - *8/1 1/2 Bleached/Dyed 250g/8.8ozs spool*
    1350 meters/1471 yards

Misti International – Misti Alpaca
PO Box 2532
Glen Ellyn, IL 60138-2532
888-776-9276
www.mistialpaca.com
info@mistialpaca.com

TUTTO Opal-Isager
505-982-8356
www.knitisager.com

Susan Upham
Halcyon Yarn
12 School St
Bath, ME 04530
800-341-0282
slu@halcyonyarn.com
Kid Seta & Douceur et Soie equivalents
for Garnstudio Kid-silk
Newport Linen 16/2

Lanaknits Designs / Hemp Yarns
Ste 3B, 320 Vernon Street
Nelson BC V1L 4E4 Canada
888-301-0011
www.lanaknits.com/usahome
info@lanaknits.com

Websites
www.dustorealpakka.com
www.tekstilmakeriet.no
www.knittingfever.com
www.diamondyarn.com
www.berroco.com
www.detmjuke.no *for Det Mjuke, Kristin*
  (100% Merino wool) 126 yds / 115 m, 50 g
www.tropicalyarns.com